China

Published in association with
Observer Research Foundation
New Delhi

Observer Research Foundation (ORF) is a public policy think-tank that aims to influence formulation of policies for building a strong and prosperous India. The ORF pursues these goals by providing informed and productive inputs, in-depth research and stimulating discussion. The Foundation is supported in its mission by a cross-section of India's leading public figures, academics and business leaders.

946

China

Economy and Environment

ORF CHINA STUDIES SERIES # 2

ACADEMIC FOUNDATION
NEW DELHI

www.academicfoundation.com

First published in 2011
by

ACADEMIC FOUNDATION
4772-73 / 23 Bharat Ram Road, (23 Ansari Road),
Darya Ganj, New Delhi - 110 002 (India).
Phones : 23245001 / 02 / 03 / 04.
Fax : +91-11-23245005.
E-mail : books@academicfoundation.com
www.academicfoundation.com

in association with the
Observer Research Foundation, New Delhi

Cataloging in Publication Data--DK
Courtesy: D.K. Agencies (P) Ltd. <docinfo@dkagencies.com>

China : economy and environment.
p. cm. -- (ORF China studies series ; 2)
Contributed articles.

ISBN 13: 9788171888948
ISBN 10: 8171888941

1. China--Economic conditions--Congresses. 2. China--Foreign economic relations--Congresses. 3. Sustainable development--China--Congresses. I. Observer Research Foundation. II. Title. III. Series: ORF China studies series ; 2.

DDC 330.951 23

Typeset by Italics India, New Delhi.
Printed and bound in India.

Contents

About the Editor/Contributors

Editor:

M. Rasgotra, President, ORF-Centre for International Relations, was decorated with the Padma Bhushan in 2002. Educated at Government College, Lahore, he joined Indian Foreign Services in September 1949. In the pioneering Indian diplomacy, he served with distinction in Indian missions in Washington D.C., Kathmandu and in the Ministry of External Affairs. From 1958 to 1962, he made a notable contribution in the evolution and implementation of India's policies towards her neighbours. His Ambassadorial career took him to Morocco and Tunisia, the USA, Britain, Nepal, the Netherlands, France and UNESCO. His tenure as Foreign Secretary (1982 to 1985) was marked by a renewal in Indo-American relations, sustained negotiations with Pakistan and a tentative opening to China. He played a significant role at the prestigious events of the Seventh Non-Aligned Summit, the Commonwealth Heads of Government Meeting, the Six-Nation Appeal on Nuclear Disarmament and the Six-Nation Summit at New Delhi.

After retirement, he was Honorary Visiting Professor, Jawaharlal Nehru University, New Delhi, Regents' Professor at University of California, Los Angeles (UCLA) and President, Delhi College of Arts & Commerce, New Delhi. He is founder President of the International Institute of Asia-Pacific Studies. Through his numerous articles, lectures and his commentaries on Indian and foreign electronic media, he continues to make an important contribution to national thinking of foreign policy and security related matters.

Contributors:

Rajeev Anantaram is Senior Fellow at Indian Council for Research on International Economic Relations (ICRIER), New Delhi. He has extensive professional experience in India and the United States, including think tanks, non-profit organisations, public interest groups and the private sector. He has worked in the areas of energy & environmental policy, technology policy and behavioural health. His research interests are in the areas of trade and investment policy regimes in South and Southeast Asia, and regional trade agreements and policies that support sustainable growth.

Vivek Bharati is Executive Director for External Affairs at PepsiCo India. Prior to this, he was advisor for national policy and programmes to Federation of Indian Chambers of Commerce & Industry (FICCI).

Prodipto Ghosh is a multidisciplinary professional specialising in the interface of science, economics and public policy. He was with the Indian Administrative Service (IAS). Currently, he is Distinguished Fellow at The Energy and Resources Institute (TERI), New Delhi. He has held many consultancy positions both in India and abroad. He has several peer-reviewed publications in the area of energy, environment and development, and several books in these fields.

Prem Shankar Jha is a noted analyst and commentator. He has written extensively for India's leading newspapers, including *The Hindu*, *The Hindustan Times*, *The Economic Times* and *The Financial Express*. He is the author of several books, including *Crouching Dragon, Hidden Tiger: Can China and India Dominate the West?* (2010).

V.P. Kharbanda is Deputy Director, National Institute of Science Technology and Development Studies, Council of Scientific and Industrial Research (CSIR), New Delhi. His research areas include technological change and innovation policies in China and India.

Sudha Mahalingam is a member of the Scientific Advisory Board of the Next Generation Infrastructures Foundation. She is an energy economist with 30 years of professional experience. She is Member of India's Petroleum and Natural Gas Regulatory Board. Her areas of interest encompass the geopolitical, economic, environmental and regulatory dimensions of all forms of energy including oil, gas, electricity including nuclear, hydro and coal as well as midstream and downstream activities like refining, petrochemicals, fertilisers etc. She has published numerous articles in Indian and international journals and writes regularly in the opinion columns of newspapers. She also speaks regularly on energy issues in national and international conferences.

Sriram Natrajan is an independent researcher currently based in Thailand. Prior to this, he was Research Professor at the Institute of Chinese Studies, Delhi. He has written extensively on rural livelihood in China.

D.S. Rajan retired as China Analyst, Cabinet Secretariat, Government of India. He was posted to Indian missions in Hong Kong, Tokyo and Beijing during service. He is presently Director of the Chennai Centre of China Studies. He has been regularly contributing articles on China to various journals and publications, besides taking part in seminars, workshops, etc.

C.V. Ranganathan has been Ambassador of India to various countries, including China and France. After his retirement from the Indian Foreign Service in 1993, he continues to be active, holding advisory and research positions. He also served as convener of the National Security Advisory Group. He has published many articles and contributions to books, newspapers, journals, and magazines in India and abroad on international affairs. He has co-authored a book entitled *India and China: The Way Ahead* (2000).

Foreword

This book is the second in the series of the Observer Research Foundation's China studies programme. China, India's great neighbour and the world's foremost rising power needs to be better understood in India, and that calls for close attention by our universities and think tanks to China's political and social evolution, its economy and how its foreign and security policies affect India and the world.

A good deal of research and writing on China has been undertaken in the United States and several countries in Europe and Asia. But we in India need to form our own object view of China's problems, policies and achievements. Of course, some good work is being done on China in some Indian universities, by scholars and former diplomats who have had direct personal experience of China: but all of it put together is far from enough. To be properly understood, this huge and powerful country, the cradle of an ancient and evolving civilisation, demands a much more sustained and methodical study. We in India need to know China better: ORF's China Studies programme is an effort in that direction.

This volume is a collection of analytical papers by Indian experts whom we brought together in a seminar at ORF on the recent performance of the Chinese economy and important related subjects, such as the food and agricultural situation, science and technological capability building, the energy picture in China and the impact of China's growth on the environment as also the external economic policies and positions it adopted after the recent global economic crisis.

The project will include China's foreign and security policies, and China's policies towards India's South Asian neighbours.

I take this opportunity to thank the authors who have contributed to this volume.

While the Foundation has encouraged freedom of expression of all points of view in this book and in its other publications, the authors alone are responsible for the facts and opinions expressed in their contributions.

—M. Rasgotra

President,
ORF Centre for International Relations

Introduction

C.V. Ranganathan

This compilation consists of the papers presented at the Seminar on China's Economy and Environment organised by ORF in July 2009. This was held in the wake of the American-led financial meltdown and its global consequences, which led to massive stimulus plans launched by the Government in China to cope with the collapse of China's export markets in the United States of America and in much of the developed countries in Europe and elsewhere. The timing was appropriate for an in-depth discussion of how the challenges of a largely export dependent model of growth could cope with the global downturn, besides to coming to terms with the several social and political challenges at home which such growth posed to through the first decade of the 21st century. Nine papers were presented on the recent performance of the Chinese economy and related important subjects such as the food and agricultural situation, science and technological capability building, and the energy picture in China. The impact of China's growth on the environment was the subject of another paper, as also the external economic policies and positions it adopted after the crisis. Lastly, there were two papers on India-China economic relations. Comparisons between various aspects of the economies of India and China were a running thread in all the papers.

The paper on 'China's Economy: Performance, Problems and Prospects: An Overview' looks at the main reasons for China's double digit growth over the two decades since 1980s and the 1990s. The move away from central decision-making down to local levels, i.e., to provinces and even lower, to townships and localities, according to the author, led to a high degree of competition between the Central and local authorities for investments in various productive as well as non-productive enterprises. Such investments, aided by bank lending, facilitated by the close nexus between the Chinese Communist Party and bank managers reached huge volumes resulting in a growth in urban incomes. On the negative side, however, there was a massive increase in capacities which far exceeded the demand for the products of investments. The net result, according to Prem Shankar Jha was that there was a state of recession in China even before the international financial crisis of 2008-09. There were other fault lines underlying the growth story which has held the world in admiration, if not awe. Some four-fifths or 80 per cent of the Chinese economy was made up of investments and exports. These investments, largely state-driven and owned, were in factories, buildings, roads, ports, power plants, railways, new airports and cumulatively contributed to exports. However such a model of economic growth led to severe imbalances leading to social unrest. A few examples of such imbalances were forcible acquisitions of land, maintenance of low wage rates, internal migration which supplied labour, environmental despoliation, inadequacy of health and social welfare measures and an unprecedented scale of corruption. In this backdrop and faced with the international financial crisis caused by the downfall of Lehman Brothers, it was not surprising that Chinese Premier Wen Jiabao reportedly said that, 'China's growth was "unstable, unbalanced, uncoordinated and unsustainable"'.

This was an honest and graphic description of the vast income disparities that had come into being where hinterland areas and particularly a great majority of rural inhabitants were not the beneficiaries of the investment-export model, massive unemployment following recession in the West, inefficient use of energy and increasing social unrest, as manifested in a vast increase in big local public demonstrations protesting for a variety of reasons. Indiscriminate investments fuelled by bank lending led to the collapse of State-controlled enterprises and spiralling bad bank loans. Lack of a universal social security net, which would provide for unemployment and health benefits discouraged domestic consumer spending, resulting in lack of demand in a situation of excess supply. Added to these were ethnic unrest and use of violence in Tibet and Xinjiang.

China's reactions to the international financial crisis have been dealt with in two separate papers which are companion pieces to the above mentioned paper. These are, 'China's External Economic Relations and Position on Leading International Economic Issues' by D.S. Rajan and a paper by C.V. Ranganathan on 'China and the Global Economic Crisis'. A stimulus package of investments pegged at US $586 billion was announced, to be invested, again in major infrastructure projects such as railways, power grids, rural assets, highways, airports and reconstruction in disaster-hit areas. Rationalisation of the industrial set up through restructuring 10 'pillar industries' has also been announced along with mergers and acquisitions of loss-making enterprises. Encouraging consumer demand through subsidies on durables, enhancing self-employment opportunities through bank lending and incentives for innovations in the energy sector are also some of the objectives for inclusion in the stimulus package. Briefly put, faced with the financial crisis, China's reactions are to implement what in Chinese experience has been a tried and tested model, namely, massive Governmental investment, more lending by banks, and creation of more inclusive infrastructure, some of which are aimed at rural areas. Results of the stimulus package after a few months have been acclaimed as helping to mitigate the worst effects of the financial meltdown and Chinese GDP was expected to register 7-8 per cent growth in 2009.

The holding of vast foreign exchange reserves, including the purchase of US Treasury bonds over the years and the potential impact these two would have on the strength of the US dollar became a major concern for both China and the USA after the crisis. It is not merely interdependence between China and the USA which had become a reality over the last two decades, but the strong dependence of the USA on Chinese domestic policies, after the crisis, which has become the major preoccupation of Finance Ministers around the world. Both China and USA have naturally a vested interest in maintaining the strength of the dollar, as the strongest currency available for investments. But over-reliance on this at a time when the USA is not showing signs of recovery from its domestic crises will be a matter of continuing concern for the Chinese. In turn the US government and some sections of big business houses frequently complain of the undervalued Chinese currency, the Yuan, which according to them help Chinese exports, cause huge trade imbalances, and impede industrial revival and employment in America.

Several proactive Chinese actions, some of which are signs of politico-economic assertiveness are listed in the two papers referred to above. These include enhanced investments abroad in the fields of resources such as energy and metals with an increasing Chinese presence in Latin America, Africa, Russia, Central Asia and Southeast Asia. The other notable initiative is the conclusion of Free Trade Agreements with regional groupings and countries in Asia.

A well researched paper on 'Food and Agriculture in China' by Sriram Natrajan illustrated by several figures and graphs follows. Even before China's reforms in the late 1970s, agriculture was incrementally integrated with the process of modern industrialisation. The importance of the agricultural sector lies not just in the sheer size and proportion of labour resources and population involved in farming and related activities for livelihoods. It also assumes importance in meeting the demands of food and nutrition for a vast population under conditions of very low per capita cultivable land and severe climatic variables.

The politically inspired disasters inflicted on the Chinese countryside on account of Mao Zedong's policies during the late 1950s and early 1960s are well documented. Less remarked is the rapid expansion of agricultural capital between 1965 and 1980 that is mostly the last decade of Mao's rule and after. During this period, it was not just production but also consumption which rose. This expansion within the framework of collective ownership of the means of production accrued to members of communes both as economic and social entitlements. In the period associated with the chaos of the Cultural Revolution (1965-1976) the mobilisation of labour to carry out rural industrialisation and agricultural mechanisation and extension of irrigation networks led to the build-up of agricultural capital.

In the early 1980s the household responsibility system was officially recognised, where individual households contracted with the authorities to meet targeted volumes of agricultural production, thus bringing the commune system to a gradual closure. The flood gates of incentives for greater individual or family rural entrepreneurship were opened. Procurement prices for agricultural produce were enhanced. Labour was released for diversification of the rural economy and a progressive decentralisation of authority and responsibility gave rise to newer forms of organisation in agriculture, industry and commerce. The acclaimed rise of township and village enterprises (TVEs) followed. Security of tenures for farming communities over land was ensured by extending lease periods, and legal recognition of farmers' rights to transfer land rights was guaranteed and a system of insurance in rural areas introduced.

Over the period from 1980-2007 cereal output has increased, recording an over 70 per cent rise in 2006 from 1980. However a diversion of land to non-cereal and commercial crops, vegetables and fruits has led to decreases in area devoted to cereal production. Another major shift in food production from the 1990s is the huge rise in animal sources of food and aquatic products. However there are also some challenges to China's food security which will have to be faced. This includes, in particular, the worsening distribution of income in all dimensions, interpersonal, inter-regional as well as rural-urban. Average nutritional availability is adequate by FAO standards, but the essential problem for food security is whether the availability translates into entitlements for the lower income deciles of the population. The diversion of farmlands towards high value crops and towards the production of food grains is a response to demands arising out of the changing composition of food consumption of higher income groups. While urban incomes have grown dramatically from the 1980s rural incomes have not kept pace, and even stagnated from that period. A sizable percentage of China's trade surplus dollars is used for agricultural imports.

The very detailed paper on 'Science and Technological Capability Building in China: Impact of Open Policies' by V.P. Kharbanda traces, with the help of figures and graphs, policy initiatives since the reform era from 1978 to contemporary times. The shift from the Mao era's concentration on research for defence, to a focus on the civilian sector in the reform era was attempted with the adoption of 'open door policies' for foreign investment and import of technologies from developed countries. A thorough reorganisation of scientific institutions and a revival of professionalism among the scientific community, *albeit* under the overall control of the Communist Party, were the other changes. Through the 1980s, a beginning was also made to bring scientific institutions closer to enterprises for commercial exploitation of indigeneous research. Programmes were initiated in areas of high technology, by the creation of technology markets and development of science and technology parks.

By the mid-1980s, there was a new policy thrust in the form of reduction of subsidies to R&D institutions so that technology markets could come into being for transactions between researchers and industrial users. A Chinese Patent Law was enacted in 1985 and revised twice (1992, 2000) thereafter. In August 1988 a programme called the Torch Plan to support and regulate new high technologies was initiated by the State Science and Technology Commission (SSTC) with the objective to develop new and high-tech products in specific zones called high technology development zones, located near universities, and research institutions with linkages to the chain of Chinese Academy of Science laboratories. At present China has 120 such institutions in specialised fields and all of them have the freedom to engage in international trade. Projects started under the Torch Plan contribute greatly to China's export earnings.

Human resource development has been treated as a priority area since the 1980s. S&T manpower has constantly increased from 0.425 million in 1952 to 5.276 million in 1980 to 28.48 million in 2002. The corresponding figure for India as of 2000 is 7.664 million. In China, over recent years R&D expenditure has increased over 10 times from US $3.45 billion in 1995 to more than US $38 billion in 2006. The corresponding figures for India are US $1.55 billion in 1995 to only US $6.62 billion in 2006. In both India and China, experience so far has shown that foreign direct investment by multinationals has not added significantly to the transfer of technologies.

The paper also covers in some detail the increasing role of venture capital in commercialising research, the build-up of linkages between universities and industry, research output in major scientific journals, and the numbers of patents filed in the USA and nationally. In all these, the Chinese score is higher than India's and the author annotates this with the help of figures.

The paper on 'China: The Energy Picture' by Sudha Mahalingam is an objective assessment of this subject. It presents some hard facts, which illuminate the problems China faces in this sector. The paper disagrees with exaggerated notions of the consequences of China's worldwide quest for acquiring energy assets. By the next 25 years China is expected to become the largest consumer of fossil fuels. In 2006, 70 per cent of China's oil consumption was accounted for by industry, 10 per cent by the commercial sector and 7 per cent by transportation. This reflects China's growth model, especially the perception that it is the factory of the world. The distribution of consumption also reveals its skewed nature, as it is the urban well-off who have a larger share of energy than the rural sector. Urbanisation and metropolitan developments contribute largely to the position China is in presently.

Another factor behind the rise of energy consumption is the vast increase of automobiles on China's roads. It is expected that at the present rate of increase in this sector, 66 per cent of oil consumption will be in the transportation sector in the next 10 years. Coal demand is rising and so is demand for natural gas. The relative low pricing of petroleum products, when compared to other Asian countries also accounts for increases in consumption. Besides, China's own oil reserves are depleting.

China is the second largest importer of fossil fuels, next only to the USA. The Persian Gulf nations provide 45 per cent, Africa 33 per cent and Russia 8 per cent. Import dependence thus makes China vulnerable to price volatility and soaring import bills. This in turn causes anxieties with regard to the security of sea lanes, stability of supplies from West Asia and domestic stability and security in areas of China's investments. In this background, China, like every other major power and regional group is doing exactly what it did, before it became a major actor on the world energy stage. In this it is facilitated by its own national oil corporations which are cash rich from the pricing and other policies adopted in China and which are in monopolistic positions at home. China's response to ensuring fossil fuel security has been through the acquisition of oil equity abroad, entering into long-term contracts and purchase of oil assets. Diversification of sources of supply also helps in diversification of transport routes lessening dependence on Southeast Asian sea routes. The other major drive undertaken by China is the laying of pipelines to leverage its geography where she shares vast land borders with producing countries such as Russia, Central and Southeast Asian countries. Mahalingam concludes that it will be difficult for China to avoid dependence on overseas imports for its energy requirements, in spite of vigorous attempts at acquisitions, leases, long-term contracts etc. The building of pipelines, greater investments in hydro power projects at home provide options but cannot replace imports. Policy reforms particularly in the pricing sector are needed as part of a more coherent energy strategy.

The paper on 'China's Challenges in Environment and Development' by Prodipto Ghosh could have more appropriately been titled, 'India and China in the Context of Climate Change Negotiations'. The similarity of the positions of the two countries in these negotiations arises from the fact that their situations with respect to various parameters affecting the environment, natural resource endowments and their respective stages of development are comparable. In spite of a higher growth trajectory over many years in China, the overarching issues of climate change are similar in nature for India and China. However the major differences lie in the scale of the changes and do not amount to major differences in perspective as to how the problems surrounding climate change are to be addressed.

A few examples, which substantiate this conclusion, would suffice. India's ecological footprint has been calculated at 6 per cent whereas China's is 16 per cent. This figure is based on assumptions which are questionable. Official figures from China estimate that ecological damage from China's growth amounts to 3.5 per cent to 7 per cent of GDP. This pulls down GDP growth, if accepted, to India's level. India may be less water-stressed than China, but in both countries the common concern is that of enforcement of laws to ensure adherence to water quality standards. In both countries there are common concerns regarding air quality with both facing pollution caused by coal-fired power stations, vehicular emissions, chemical plants etc. India has a larger population without access to electricity. In both countries the energy sector accounts for the highest volumes of greenhouse gas emissions. China's energy intensity is decreasing at a much lower rate than India's. Fifty-three per cent of India's power generation depends on coal, and in China's case it is 78 per cent. In availing of the Clean Development Mechanism (set up under the Kyoto Protocol) China has overtaken India, occupying the first position, while India is just behind.

Dealing with the subject of contentious negotiations over climate change issues, the author outlines the positions taken by the 'Annex I' countries (developed countries) and 'Annex II' (developing countries). The wide range of differences between the two groups of countries arises broadly speaking from lack of a consensus on a long-term vision for addressing climate change. This feature overshadows the details of the substance of the negotiations. The author goes into details which show that the gap between the Annex I countries and the Annex II countries could well nigh be unbridgeable unless political wills are exercised to find equitable solutions.

Finally there are two papers with identical titles, 'India-China Economic Relations' by Vivek Bharti and Rajeev Anantaram. Understandably they cover the same ground; both reach pessimistic conclusions about India's ability to narrow or close the trade deficit with China. This has grown over the years even as China has become India's largest trade partner and India figures as China's seventh largest partner. That such large trade deficits against India are unsustainable is a point made *ad nauseam* by businessmen and by Government Ministers and officials from India in meetings with Chinese counterparts. It is unlikely however that India will find early solutions to this problem.

Nearly 60 per cent of Indian exports to China in 2009 which amounted to nearly US $14 billion (as against a total turnover of US $43 billion) is dominated by primary or by very low labour-intensive products. China's export basket to India is diversified, reflecting its wide manufacturing base comprising both labour and capital-intensive items, and both high-tech and high value items. This is in keeping with China's emergence as an energetic globaliser aiming at the markets of developed countries in contrast with the approach of Indian business to aim at the domestic market.

The other aspect worth pondering is that China's growth and its manufacturing-export model has facilitated an integrated business-economic architecture in Southeast and East Asia, which in turn feeds into China's export performance. Components, sub-assemblies produced in the ASEAN region in Japan and South Korea are worked upon in China and re-exported to the world. In fact China's trade with this region shows a negative trade balance. This integration will be further cemented when the free trade regions between China and regional groups and individual countries are agreed upon. It is clear that India too would have to try vigorously to become a part of the Asian supply chain if it hopes to add more value added items to its basket. Both papers highlight the importance of bringing about structural changes in the industrial scene in India and suggest various measures for changing the focus from being essential domestically driven to export oriented. There are detailed analyses of the commodities which figure in the two-way trade between India and China which substantiate the authors' claims about the unsustainable nature of India's exports to China unless there are major changes in the equation.

Some concluding observations are in order which supplement the papers presented at the Seminar. The Chinese economic model seems to have been pitched outside the framework either of derived wisdom of economists or conventional economics as experienced elsewhere. There is no other example, perhaps, of such huge scales and sizes of state investments and resultant foreign exchange earnings from exports. In China's case, size matters as also the historically unprecedented prosperity of a large percentage of its vast population. It now remains to be seen how soon and quickly China can substitute or supplement its past growth model with sufficient domestic initiatives to boost consumption and bring about a more acceptable level of equity. Political initiatives are also required to bring about the social harmony to which all Chinese aspire. Protectionism in the West and the contentious value of the Chinese currency are issues that could well overshadow the quality of China's economic engagement with it.

On the environmental front, more attention needs to be paid by us to the huge investments China is making in non-conventional sources of energy such as nuclear, solar, wind, biomass, etc. Currently Chinese investments in these areas exceed those made by other countries. This shows that the regime in China is fully aware of its responsibilities to reduce the deficits that have resulted from its past search for growing GDP at the cost of the environment.

On India-China economic relations a major exercise of political will is called for in China to balance the trade baskets given the size and importance of bilateral trade in both countries. Within India the Government, businessmen and industrialists must seriously work at adding more high value and high-tech items to India's export basket.

1 China's Economy: Performance, Problems and Prospects

An Overview

Prem Shankar Jha

China has been treading a tight rope between growth and its social consequences, and is now in danger of falling off. That does not of course mean that they do not know this. In fact, they are very aware of the danger. It is also not true that they cannot do anything about it. However, course correction would mean a departure from, not just the ethos of the Communist Party, but more than 2,000 years of Confucian hardwiring of their genes. This is what China is finding nearly impossible at the moment.

This paper is not concerned only with China's economic growth. What I am really interested in dealing with is, how China's political economy functions, and in particular, try to explain two anomalies about China's growth which are not adequately understood. First, how is it possible that a country with the highest growth rate that the world has ever known by far, can also have a phenomenally high rate of political discontent? China's growth rate has been almost 10 per cent by official estimates, and indeed, exceeding 10 per cent for more than 31 years. The number of mass protests grew from 8,700 in 1993, according to President Hu Jintao's own revelations, to 87,000 in 2005. (Note that when the Chinese talk about 'mass protests', these are nothing less than confrontations against the Chinese state.) This 'Blue Book' for 2007 says the number of protests has gone up to more than 80,000, but it will no longer spell out what these protests were all about. Another journal referred to a lower, more restrained number. One notes that in 2006, the number of mass protests went up to over 90,000.

The second anomaly is: how is it that an economy that has a constant trade surplus, the largest free foreign exchange reserves in the world, by a huge margin—and therefore the most phenomenal base in the entire world for political and economic power—remains inefficient? Forget about comparing China's rates of consumption of energy and raw materials, which is probably the true measure of efficiency; forget about comparing China with the US or Europe, where economic systems are different. Simply compare it with India: China's consumption of raw materials per dollar of GDP growth is three times as that of India, and their consumption of energy is 2.2 times higher.

I shall try and explain these anomalies. First of all, let us take the growth rate, which has been much discussed i.e., whether China's high growth rate is an artificial, contrived figure—or is it that as a figure it is too low, and that the real growth rate is actually higher. These anomalies about China's growth rate arise from the fact that the system of reporting such growth—is a self-reporting system. Every enterprise, big or small, is obliged to report performance. Until about 1995-96, this was just a routine economic reporting system. It was around 1996 that the reporting system got politicised, as Jiang Zemin and Zhu Rongji began to lay down targets for the economy in the following year. Everyone who is a decision-maker at any level of the Chinese economy is also a Party member, and they are competing with each other. The reporting system unleashed a competition to show who was doing better, leading to a steady inflation of data. In 2005, when a detailed economic census of China was conducted, the National Bureau of Statistics concluded that the average inflation of GDP data in China was 3.6 per cent. Even before that Census, the authorities already knew this to be the case. At that time their practice was to make certain ad hoc corrections to the data that streamed in from the provinces. However, this time they created a really solid base, with 30,000 people in the field to carry out the Census, which took up most of that year.

Why did this not happen earlier than 1996-97? The basic reason is that in 1996, China fell into a huge recession and the leadership refused to acknowledge it. The first to bring this to attention of the international community was Thomas G. Rawski, a well-known economist. He pointed out that it was not possible to register a 7 per cent or 8 per cent growth rate over three years with a 12 per cent decline in energy consumption.

Rawski's analysis set off an uproar in the China studies fraternity. Much to his surprise, he was criticised by the American economic establishment including China watchers and economists. He was even attacked by a leading China research institute in Russia. He was so horrified at the reaction to his thesis, that he began to backtrack. Rawski had said that the growth in China in at least two of the four years which he covered, that is, between 1997 and 2000—was as low as 2 per cent. A variety of studies soon followed, mostly based upon consumption-based reports which also showed China's growth rates falling very sharply to as low as 4 per cent in the said period. However, China simply did not acknowledge any of this. That period showed exactly what the problem with self-reporting is: once it is made competitive, then the reported growth rates will keep getting inflated. Further, this works asymmetrically: if production has gone up, it will most certainly be reported, but if it has declined then it will not be. Chinese official data on the upswings can be given credence but data on the downswings are to be suspected. If those specific five years (1996-2001, or the full period of the recession) are taken into account, China's annual growth rate may be pulled down by about 1 per cent or 0.8 per cent over the active period of 30 years. This still leaves them, however, with a phenomenal growth rate.

One also needs to note another consequence of the self-reporting system: China's GDP is underreported. Even today it is underreported i.e., the real GDP is higher than what they are proclaiming. We are talking about the absolute GDP, not the rate of growth of the GDP. The reason is that an increasing proportion of the Chinese economy has been privatised, and as a larger part of the privatised section of the economy comprises individual entrepreneurship—at all levels, from the food cart vendor to the individual computer technologist working from home—the normal human tendency of trying to minimise under-declaration of one's income in order to reduce one's tax burden, is very much in evidence and if anything, is amplified in China. A Chinese economist had actually pointed this out at a time when there was a controversy about people underreporting their incomes i.e., that China's GDP growth rate is even faster than the published figure. But this component which was virtually non-existent till the mid-1990s, is now quite substantial. The Chinese government made a correction following the Census, which included many sectors that had not been taken into account earlier. Now China has come out with its own set of independent studies which point to an increase in GDP estimate by at least 30 per cent. These were not tricks which China is sometimes accused of; the fact is that this is a much bigger economy than it appears to be. A significant implication is that if India has an adversarial relationship with China, then the Chinese economy also implies a threat to India.

What is the reason for China's high growth? The winding up of centralised planning between 1981 and 1983, and the transfer of investment decisions down to six levels of local government from the provinces down to the townships—and even to village-level administrations—resulted in something that no one could have foreseen, but was very welcome in China in the early stages of this process. It was the competition between two emerging classes of capitalists. You can call them a 'crypto-bourgeoisie' because they have not really yet become part of the bourgeois mainstream. There is competition between Central investing authorities and the local, in the broad sense between the Centre and every level, from the provincial down to the township investing authorities (in all there are almost 100,000 investing authorities in China). This competition is inherent in the monolithic system of the Communist Party, but it also arose from the fact that once holding private wealth or income was no longer deemed to be a crime and that you could legally accumulate wealth, corruption entered the scene in a big way. This corruption has been described *ad nauseam* in the literature on China, so one does not need to elaborate. The important thing is that it was the beginning of the delegitimisation of the Communist system which was the main reason for protest at Tiananmen. The Tianenmen democratic movement was not intended to facilitate a further leap towards western-style capitalism; it was intended to facilitate the exact opposite. It was a last despairing effort by the losers from this process to bring some control into it by using the democratic process: accountability. This is however a new theme needing detailed examination.

What this competition has done is interesting. At every level, investment projects were thought of and executed, because at every level the local Party secretary outranked the Bank manager, and the entire savings of the Chinese citizenry were at his disposal. More than 80 per cent of the savings of the Chinese people are held to date, by state-owned banks. So all you had to do was to think of a project, ring up the Bank manager, and say 'produce the money, please'. Over the years, Beijing has tried to regulate this in a variety of ways. There have been a series of reforms—taxation reform in 1994, banking reform in 1998, another round of taxation reform in 1997-98, repeated in 2002, and 2006—all of which were implemented in order to retain control over resources because, conferred to a handful of Ministries in Beijing, there were thousands of investing centres in Beijing and in the provinces. If you take just township and village administration there are more than 60,000 and were all vying for a share in the same cake, admittedly, a huge cake i.e., savings in the banks.

The good side of such competition was that it led to huge increases in investment, and consequently growth rates that were unimaginable. The statements and national growth targets coming out of Beijing between 2004 and 2007 were emphatic in calling for a slowing down of the growth rate, not for speeding up. China's bugbear has been growth that is too fast, and cannot be controlled. It is like an engine in which the regulators have been lost (or perhaps they never were there, to begin with). The reason why Hu Jintao, in particular, took up the issue was because he finally admitted what Jiang Zemin and Zhu Rongji and the entire post 1989 generational leadership refused to admit: i.e., the growth of this kind is leading to political discontent, and that such discontent would explode when the growth slowed down. The trouble with this kind of growth where investment can take place without any real control, with so many people involved, and when it is totally outside the control of market forces, is that you are going to get huge investments. While the investment is taking place, incomes will be growing, and so will be consumption; this will work, but a moment arrives when you have over-invested your capacity far in excess of demand, and suddenly you find that you cannot sell anything. The crash that comes is so huge in absolute terms that they have to keep it concealed, which is exactly what happened in 1997.

This is precisely what the leadership fears i.e., that every time it happens, there is a great increase in political discontent. The problems brought by the growth pattern apart from the delegitimisation resulting from corruption are: above all unemployment—stated telegraphically, it means that unemployment rises when there is recession. Companies or enterprises which are making money stops making money and start losing. This loss has to be absorbed by the state budget, because contrary to what people have been saying—'Ah! China is doing so well because it is going to the market, it is privatising and so on'—even today, less than half of the economy of China is privatised. This proportion includes the entire joint venture and export sector. If you look at the basic internal economy, the private sector is probably not much more than 20 per cent. All investment is done under the State's auspices and the State remains the main entrepreneur, *albeit* a multi-level, hydra-headed entrepreneur. Local governments invested hugely during the first period of decontrol. Between 1978 and 1996, the number of centrally-owned state enterprises went up by 30,000, and the number of locally-owned state enterprises went up by 7.87 million. What happened when the recession hit, was that the vast bulk of these 7.87 million enterprises became loss-makers. Instead of adding to the revenues of the State governments, they became a huge drain. Yet the administrative responsibility of the State governments did not decline. What is more, the recession hit two years after a huge tax reform in 1994—which was actually expropriation, whereby the proportion of all tax revenues spent at the local levels was brought down to 30 per cent. But the Centre did not reduce the provincial governments' administrative duties; on the contrary, it got increased. Until that point they were only required to provide for five years of education for children; it was then increased to nine years. This meant that you had to find the teachers, you had to build the schools, you had to get the books, practically you had to do everything, and all this had to be done out of your budget! Thus the requirement to spend increased, while the money available decreased. They invested hugely in small enterprises of all kinds believing that there was never a downturn. When the downturn came, that money disappeared. As a result, from 1996 onwards, there was a huge spate of forced privatisation. These million enterprises were simply given away to the workers. That is what the whole western world applauded: 'Look at China, it is going the privatisation way.' In fact, there has been no change in the objective of the leadership; it is not to relinquish control, but to hold on to power by any means.

How then did the local authorities meet their commitments with a much smaller revenue base? This they did by levying a whole series of local taxes, fees and fines. These levies multiplied at a phenomenal rate and both Chinese commentators and foreign analysts have said that, at one point, the average villager was paying 149 separate taxes and fees. Over and above this, there were fines. This was like squeezing the peasants in any way possible to get money out of them, in order to carry out the goals of the local governments. This led to increased discontent, eventually leading to the tenfold rise in protests that we discussed earlier. Indeed, the indication is of a state of continuous popular discontent against government.

The current recession, is something that China is willing to admit perhaps because it has coincided with the global economic downturn. In 1997, China did admit to a slowdown, as it also coincided with a larger pattern in the East Asian region. In fact, the Chinese economy was at that point so insulated from the regional crisis, that the little impact was limited. This is no longer the case i.e., the impact of the global economic crisis on China is substantial.

There is a huge corpus of data—showing that the recession caused by excess investment had already begun in 2007. In some industries, the downturn started even earlier. For example, in 2004, as much as 48 per cent of all automobiles being manufactured in China remained unsold even by November. Overall, as the World Bank has pointed out, the ratio of unsold finished goods to total production had risen to 15 per cent by early 2005. At the height of the 1997-2000 recessions, that ratio was 17.8 per cent. It had come very close to a point where over-investment would give the economy a huge downward dip; and that downward dip began long before the global recession. A number of steel plants had to be mothballed on the very day they were set up. There are several of these plants across the country that have not produced even one tonne of steel, just as there are about 130 automobile plants that do not produce a single automobile. In early 2009, it was estimated that 90 million tonnes of iron-ore were sitting idly in the ports. Steel plants were not prepared to accept this iron-ore because they did not have enough production orders. There is abundant evidence that China was going into this downturn: then came the global recession, which had slashed their export sector and badly hit employment.

China, unlike India, wants to know what is happening. They have done an endless number of surveys, for example, that 25 million out of the 82 million people who worked in the Yangtze Delta region were migrant workers who were not able to find jobs. Half of them stayed behind in the villages, and half came back to towns, and had not found jobs by the end of March. Those who stayed in the villages have had their land allocation given away. Hence there were conflicts at the village level. A Contract Law amendment was announced (January, 2008) to take care of this dire situation, in which as many as 25 million families lost their incomes and were sent home.

The Chinese government is fully aware of all the dangers here. Over and above this, they happen to face a huge surplus in productive capacity. What do they do? They implement their economic revival programme (i.e., the revival package with 4 trillion Yuan or 583 billion US dollars.) And the whole world said, 'Oh! It is impossible.' 'The dragonomists'—the economists of such organisations—said that only one-third of this amount is in fact new and that the stimulus fund does not really amount to US $583 billion. There is a reliable index of how much is actually being implemented. This revival plan was unveiled in November 2008; in the January to March quarter of 2009, bank lending increased over the same period in 2008 by 4.6 trillion Yuan, all of which was investment. Where is this investment going? Fifty per cent of it was for transport and power; 12 per cent for rural village infrastructure; 12 per cent for shoring up the environment and protecting natural areas; 9 per cent for affordable housing, technology and restructuring; 5 per cent for modernisation of industry; and 1 per cent for health and education. In reality there is a lot more which is hidden under other heads. Why? Because this is the only way you can use the plants and enterprises that you have set up, it is the only way you can use the facilities you have created. We should keep in mind that China is an infrastructure-led economy. Here is where the problem really arises i.e., the political problem. The incomes of provincial governments would go down sharply, as they depend on only one tax which is the business tax, and that business tax is levied on local enterprises as distinct from taxes levied by the Centre. These are the ones worst hit by recession and so the revenue is going to drop sharply. It is the same problem they faced in 1997. The difference is that they no longer have to collect fees and local taxes; all these have been taken away. No one knows what they are going to do and how they are going to do it. What the Central government did to get this huge jump in investment was to go back to the old planning system, and they asked all the state-level and local-level people to give them a list of projects that they wanted to implement. By early December, they had a list of projects worth 25 trillion Yuan, and they had to cherry-pick among them the best projects. Typically, unlike India, China went ahead immediately to implement this idea. (In India, we first appoint an expert committee, and then another panel, and then another expert committee and then the bureaucracy sits on the final panel's recommendations, waters it down and then three years later you will get some action.) What China did was to ask the entrepreneur to borrow from the banks, the State would give you the tranches later. An extra-low level interest facility was created, which allowed them to borrow unlimited amounts. The local enterprises acted well ahead of the Centre which, in any case, committed to only giving one-third of the total investment. Thus, they have gone to the banks, got the money, and started investing. However 90 per cent of this investment is in infrastructure. These are labour-light and materials-heavy investments, and everything that is produced here comes from the cities. What this means is you are borrowing from the banks, from the savings of the people, and then transferring the money to the cities. Whatever growth there is, will take place in the cities, and it is going to be directly at the expense of shifting the savings of the rural population once again into the cities. This is not new; it has been going on in China for 2,000 years. There is no doubt that sooner or later this is going to lead to an intense reaction in the rural areas, however delayed.

All this has implication for international relations also. Historically, China has dealt with this kind of internal unrest through the hyping up of Chinese nationalism. This has again been in evidence i.e., in the manner of dealing with the restiveness breaking out in the far-flung areas, in Tibet in 2008, and among the Uighurs in 2009. This interest is likely to move towards the Centre as time goes by. The leadership has discovered a 'powerful' tool in nationalism. If you combine Chinese nationalism with the need to maintain legitimacy and growing popular discontent as a result of economic growth, they could easily go back to the 9 per cent growth rate by the end of 2010; then we are directly in their path. The threat to India from China's internal dynamics is perhaps not adequately understood.

I shall now weave into this analysis, other aspects such as sectoral development, labour, human resources, democracy and demography, and their inter-relationship, and with some comparisons between China and India that should, I hope, put an end to any complacency on our part.

Andrew G. Walder (formerly at the University of Hong Kong) presented a paper in 2006 in which he said that anybody in China who is discontented belongs to the politically or socially marginalised groups. Therefore, by definition, if the politically and socially empowered groups are happy, then no matter what happens by way of the discontent, it will not be regime threatening. There are two points that we have to bear in mind in this regard. There is an implicit assumption here that discontent is in some way a function of poverty or even, for that matter, of relative poverty, if not absolute poverty. There is a considerable literature on the theme that this connection is weak at best, and sometimes the exact opposite; we should not therefore take it seriously. It is when people start getting better off that they start asking for not simply food and assurances of a job tomorrow, but also for empowerment, to have a voice in decision-making on issues that concern their future. It is precisely at this point that they come up against opposition, as happens in an authoritarian State, or even in a democratic set up such as ours. The reaction is often delayed.

A good example of this is provided by the developments in Tibet. Mr. N. Ram, of *The Hindu* has been telling that Tibet is a paradise, and that any one out there who is disaffected is some kind of a reactionary. The truth is it is precisely because there is economic growth and development in Tibet, that it is possible for them to get together and start expressing themselves. It is taking place with the help of the internet and the mobile phone that are linking the Tibetans right across the world into a kind of virtual nation; in this manner, the threat to China is steadily growing. China is not taking it lightly, as was shown in the way they cracked down in Tibet in 2009. Now we have a similar problem concerning the Uighurs, who share tense relations with the Han (Chinese) in Sinkiang (officially Uighur Autonomous Region). One recalls an interesting remark by a Han woman being interviewed on television: 'Our Government has done so much, we have created a paradise. We have created a paradise, why are these people trying to destroy it?' Exactly the same thing was said in Tibet in 2008, and if you saw the outpourings over the internet at that time, it was seen that people were provoked on that occasion and, the authorities in

China put direct blame on India for sheltering the people who they said were provoking the Tibetans in China. The Chinese fail to understand that behind this lies a deep philosophical divide between them and the rest of the world. The essence of Confucianism is that the virtuous ruler deserves absolute obedience. If he is truly virtuous, he will not need even a police force because each one of his subjects will obey him. If you are a virtuous ruler and you do everything for the good of your subjects, and they still turn against you, then they are vicious and they go outside the pale and thus deserve to be destroyed. It seems that this is the absolute core idea and it is well over 2,000 years old and nothing has changed in that. If you see the reactions towards the Tibetans in 2008, and the Uighurs in 2009, they fall exactly into the same pattern. China does not have any other way of dealing with dissent other than the Confucian recipe! 'Give them more and they will be happy. Get them justice, give them this, and give them that'. The point is that essentially from top to bottom. This system is breaking down in central China and it is not accepted by two major 'ethnic' communities. These are the twin sources of political threat in China.

Another basic question is that of reviving domestic consumption when there is no national market. To some extent, China compensates for this by having a highly decentralised system of investment decision-making by the State, hence the importance of the proposals for projects totalling 25 trillion Yuan, every single township and village administration has been asked to put forth. To the extent that they are approved and the fact that they will proceed, whether or not they get the 'go-ahead' or not, this involves a great display of energy and turbulence, both positive and negative. The positive aspect is that, this is going to be a broad-based revival package and will help. Further, there is a national market as was seen in the case of the great famine of 1958-1961. There is evidence, that not only are people buying products from across the country, but also that every local government has been doing its best to tax these trans-border transactions to extract revenue from them. Thus, it is a very imperfect national market beset with many problems. However, these problems are not insurmountable.

Another related point is that China's capital output ratio is now considerably higher than that of India, partly because of the wasteful nature of investment. There is massive duplication of investment taking place in China as a result of its decentralised investment decision-making. If further corrections are made for the possibility that China's overall growth rate is 1 per cent lower than what they officially claim or 0.8 per cent lower than the capital output ratio, then the difference between India and China on this index becomes even bigger. As of 2006, it was 4.21 in India and 4.521 in China; now it could easily be 4.821. What is important is that this development began manifesting itself post 1996. The capital output ratio was relatively low, and energy efficiency correspondingly high in the 1980s. That was when most of the development of township and village enterprises (TVEs) took place. Mostly the investments went into consumer goods, enabling immediate consumption with a fixed quota for the domestic market. The benefits were widespread, perhaps accounting for the absence of political dissent until the mid-1990s. It is said that in 1993, for example, the average protest action against state authority involved no more than six people. By 2005, this figure had gone up to 60. That phase ended, and there was a brief recession in 1989-90, followed by a huge opening up. All of a sudden everybody was making investments, and getting rich was seen as a good thing. There was a phenomenal growth and the capital output ratio increased rapidly, and so did materials intensity and energy intensity. Even this was nothing compared to what happened after 1997, because simultaneously a large part of the labour-intensive smaller industries were set up all across the country and the township and village administrations went broke. It is estimated that more than two million of these out of 7.87 million industries had become insolvent. But the reforms that took place in 1994, first in the taxation system, and in 1997 in the banking system—which transferred control of both bank resources, and in particular, of tax revenues resources to the Central government from the State governments—encouraged the Central government to go in for large-scale projects, most of them in infrastructure. This was justified on the ground that it was necessary to fight the recession. While China never admitted to the outside world that there was a recession, the statements made by Prime Minister Zhu Rongji and President Jiang Zemin in September 1997 and March 1998 in the National People's Congress and the Party Conference, respectively, gave the world a hint of the seriousness of China's economic situation at that time. Then they went in for heavy infrastructure investment, worth some 18 billion dollars a year, and this was continued all the way up to 2004-05. Of course, infrastructure development in China was absolutely phenomenal at that time, consisting of large projects like airports and roads. What were the principal material inputs for infrastructure development? These were steel, cement, heavy earth-moving machinery, and machinery that makes that machinery—all of which were produced in relatively modern plants located in towns. Therefore the workers were required to be in towns, and those who wanted those jobs had to go there as migrant labourers. The number of China's migrant labourers went up from 80 million in the mid-1990s to some 225 million at present, (if you count townships within intra-district movement).

This kind of investment led to a concentration of income in the urban areas. This was financed through borrowing from the banks. There was an attempt to stop this trend in 1997: bank managers were told they were no longer responsible to the local Party secretary, but rather to the bank manager at the next higher level of authority, whether it is a county, a prefecture, or a province. This system never worked, though, because they all belonged to the same Party and the local Party secretary was always powerful. In the end, ways would be found around this. What has happened with this recession today, is that, even the tacit or the attempted control of the use of bank funds has been formally withdrawn. Every local authority has been granted a *carte blanche* to go to the banks and take whatever money it needs, provided only that the projects they have submitted have been approved. This again is not an absolute guidance. In the first three months of the year, the quantum of bank lending was 4.6 trillion Yuan. Incremental increases took place thereafter. Where was the money coming from? There was movement from savings accumulated in the rural areas (where the savings rate is high) into production for increasing incomes and creating employment in the towns. Thus the inequalities between town and country are going to keep growing and this is something China has to deal with. There was the idea that dissent is local and is therefore capable of being isolated. This has been the essential strategy of every 'Confucian' government for the last 2,000 years, and they had elaborate systems for this. You did have the right of appeal against local authority called the 'right of rightful resistance'. This system has broken down today. The grievances office in Beijing gets as many as two million petitions a year, and just cannot cope with this number. People who have braved the wrath of local authorities after having failed at every level with the local government to get any kind of restitution have ended up in Beijing with their petitions, and still unable to get to meet the grievance office. So great is the difficulty of getting in; it is said that only people who have come with petitions live here because they cannot go back. As there have been cases where the returnees have been killed because the issue they protested against was not a tax or a fee, which are the only issues that they are used to. They may not like it, and they will make verses and songs out of it, but they will not actually take up cudgels against injustice and that is what they are not getting a remedy for. This became a very serious problem and part of the reason why President Hu Jintao radically changed the focus of policy in 2004. Therefore, internal isolation is breaking down—for example, because of the internet and the humble telephone. These are being monitored with increasing thoroughness. Just recently there was a decision to insert a customised software into computers in order to make sure that every time anyone gets online, the controlling authority has the right to take off sites at will, (and if one tries to get on the line, the interactions will be recorded). The methods of control is leading to developing technologies beyond anything that George Orwell had even remotely imagined when he wrote his classic novel, *1984*. Very recently, the Central government banned Uighurs from going to mosques. How long is this system going to last? The case of the Falun Gong is instructive. The point is that 10,000 members of the gang could arrive in Beijing without the authorities knowing about it. Thus their capacity to isolate and control through monitoring was breaking down. Another constituency which has emerged in China is that of disillusioned Party cadres, educated villagers and some ex-servicemen who are now giving their services to villages, migrant workers, and so on, to plead their cases and become the mobilisers. Many have been killed off. Nonetheless, their numbers are increasing.

Then there is a very strong demand for civil society that is emerging in China, particularly in the cities. When the Shanghai mayor or Party secretary who was eventually jailed—decided that he would extend the Maglev train at a cost of US $5.5 billion—there was so much public anger and the Party Committee had to meet under the same security protection that was given to visiting State dignitaries. When he was sacked, firecrackers went off all over Shanghai.

Do they ever worry about profitability or viability of capital expenditure? One example will suffice. The payback period of the Maglev train between Shanghai and Bu Dong, which everybody is so thrilled about, is presently calculated at 167 years. No further comment is needed on the rentability of this project. The Tibetan Railway and the Three Gorges Dam project are also leading examples of projects that will not pay for themselves. Hu Jintao has taken these problems into account and the 'social harmony' concept has been effective to some degree. It has been said that most of the predatory behaviour is limited to the local government level. Most of their powers have been taken away. However this act remains a top downwards operation and is based on the same model of huge infrastructure development, which has created the social discontent, to begin with. The remedy is not difficult to find. China could do what it did in 1978 i.e., raise the price of food grains (which is controlled by the government), and change the terms of trade in favour of agriculture; then increased rural income will flood the entire countryside with little effort on the part of the state. The catch is that this process will make all these huge infrastructure projects even more expensive. In fact this is what the leadership wants to do. There seems to be a systematic point about feeding the towns at the expense of the countryside which has been the downfall of every Chinese dynasty in the last 2,000 years; we are seeing the same thing being repeated.

There are a few other things that can be done, including introducing democratic empowerment. In fact, this approach is summed up in a book produced by the Central Party School, called the *15-year Assault*, which is a programme for democratising from the grassroots upwards. However, 15 years is too slow, and the action contemplated is very limited. One must concede that the leadership is at least aware of what is to be done. There is the imperative, for example, of a separate judiciary. The dominant trend seems to be a nervousness caused by rapid growth and discontent caused by the slowing down of growth in 2007, followed by the global recession. Apparently, all this has made the Chinese Central administration tighten up even more. This is a wrong reaction.

When we speak of India and China, we are really talking about David and Goliath, except that David has no slingshot. In absolute size, China's industry is 6.5 times that of India. One indication of this is infrastructure development. In 2006, India's coal-based power production capacity was 80,000 MW and overall capacity was 120,000 MW. China's coal-based power capacity was 484,000 MW, i.e., over five times India's. Since 2006, China has added a further 90,000 MW. In short, the increase that year in China's generation capacity in thermal power exceeded the whole of India's thermal power generating capacity. It is this infrastructure heavy investment that has made it possible for China to attract every company that wants to lower its costs of production. Chinese exports have actually grown between 2001 and 2006 by 400 per cent. This was because it was in this period, that leading Asian economies such as Taiwan and Korea began to run out of labour (and not merely cheap labour) and were compelled to move their last stage manufacture into China. They went to China not only because it was close but also because the required infrastructure was already there, and was excellent. In contrast, India has invested virtually nothing in infrastructure. Capital investment, whether in the maintenance of existing infrastructure or new infrastructure is no more than Rs. 5,000 crore or US $1 billion. The equivalent figure for China is US $500 billion. That is the comparison to keep in mind. On the other hand, our consumption increase is going to be on Plan and non-Plan together, i.e., Rs. 300,000 crore—this is the increased spending that is designed to boost consumption. So we are going to spend money consumption without producing, and without putting anything in by way of infrastructure, that is the wherewithal with which industry can produce. Just compare the two countries, and ask yourselves what the future holds. China will become unstable because it is growing too fast with the wrong kind of investment. We are becoming unstable because we are not investing enough, but also doing the wrong kind of consumption.

References

Walder, G. Andrew (2007). "Social Stability and Popular Protest in China: How Serious is the Threat?", Paper presented at the International Conference on Contemporary China, University of Hong Kong, January 5-6, (2007).

2 Food and Agriculture in China

Sriram Natrajan

Introduction

Despite the mega transformations that China has undergone in the past five to six decades in its social and economic institutional structures, and in the quantum as well as the composition of material production, agriculture in particularly the rural economy continues to occupy a central position. 'Agriculture as the foundation', was the cornerstone of China's development strategy since the 1950s, and till today the status of this sector has not diminished in significance, as evident from the deliberations at the Third Plenum of the 17th Party Congress of the Chinese Communist Party Central Committee (CCPCC).[1] Besides reaffirming the need to safeguard farmers' rights and interests, the Plenum also called for the consolidation and strengthening of the fundamental status of agriculture.

In the period prior to new institutional reforms launched at the end of the 1970s, the rural economy as a whole was incrementally integrated with the processes of modern industrialisation identified with economic development and growth. Since the late 1980s this sector was additionally integrated at a rapid pace with the global economy. The centrality of the agricultural sector in China's development strategy rests not only on the sheer size and proportions of labour resources and population, involved in farming and related activities for livelihood, but also on the importance of this sector in meeting the demands of food and nutrition for a large and expanding population under conditions of very low per capita cultivable

1. The principal items of debate at this Plenum held in Beijing on 9-12 October 2008, were rural reform and rural development. The major draft document that formed the background to the discussion on the new challenges and problems facing both the agricultural and the rural sector was 'Decision of the CCP Central Committee on Several Major Issues of Advancing Rural Reform and Development'. For a detailed report on the Third Plenum, see China Quarterly (1, 2009).

land, and severe climate and other related factors that regularly afflict farming. It is in both these contexts, that this paper examines some issues in China's agriculture.

This paper is organised as follows: Section I recounts two opposing characterisations of China's agriculture in a historical perspective. Section II details the significance of China's agrarian transformation. Here the institutional reforms in agriculture in the late 1970s (widely termed as 'decollectivisation') are presented as part of a sequence of institutional transition initiated from the mid-1960s. Section III briefly describes the changing patterns of agricultural production since the early 1980s. Section IV examines the evolution of food balances and composition since 1980 using statistical data compiled by Food and Agricultural Organization (FAO). The paper concludes with some observations on one of the serious consequences of the development path that China has embarked in the era of continuing economic reforms and high rates of growth, namely the issue of food security.

Characterising Chinese Agriculture

Until the early 1950s, China was predominantly an agrarian society with over 80 per cent of the population (over 500 million in 1953) residing in rural areas. This proportion is most likely to have been the long-term average for several centuries. Historical materials in the form of administrative documents at various levels of the state apparatus going back to over 500 years, besides treatises on agriculture dating back to over 1,000-1,500 years, have enabled scholars to compile and examine the broad features and tendencies of Chinese agrarian evolution. A pioneering work in this regard is that of Perkins (1969) that evaluates Chinese agricultural development over 600 years. One of its main findings is that at least until about the mid-20th century, the expansion in food production was such, as to maintain or even exceed living standards. This was achieved almost entirely, given the severe limitations on expanding cultivable land, by constant innovation, development and application of traditional methods/technology.[2]

---

2. Traditional methods refer to the set of all those practices and potentialities such as increasing cultivated areas as well areas sown, devising and programming the combination and sequence of crop rotation that prevents soil stress, developing

contd...

Perkins draws attention to a crucial factor that necessitated increased priority to agriculture, in particular grain production during the early decades of the People's Republic of China—namely a shift from the six-centuries average annual population growth of one per cent, to two per cent in the 1950s and the 1960s.[3] In the early 1960s, adoption of modern technology in agriculture became inevitable once the possibilities of traditional means of increasing output and the potential of collectively organised production were exhausted or were declining.

A contrarian view can be found in Huang (1990), in which agricultural systems are classified into three categories defined by the capacity to break through the barrier of productivity over long periods of time. Agricultural systems are therefore, either 'developmental' where productivity and income increases are achieved, 'intensive' when productivity is maintained or 'involutionary' in which productivity and income increases are close to zero or falling in average terms. China in this view belonged to the last category for more than 600 years until the early 1980s. Accordingly, in the initial period following the founding of the People's Republic of China agriculture continued to be 'involutionary', even though institutionally distinct ('Collectivist involution'), when despite the system did not transit to a 'developmental' state as labour productivity, and income per day stagnated despite expansion in output during 1950-1980.[4] In this view therefore, collective agriculture did not achieve productive efficiency and

---

...contd...

higher quality fertilisers, improving seed selection procedures and practices, collating and distributing dispersed knowledge widely in all the above aspects for testing and making further improvements and above all improving and maintaining water control systems which occupies a central position in rice agriculture. In Perkins' view, beyond the mid-20th century, traditional agriculture in the face of a physical limit to cultivated land could not have achieved the necessary growth to keep pace with the shift in the demographically induced demand.

3. According to his estimates, between the 14th and the 19th centuries, population and grain output rose six times and by about 50 per cent in the first half of the 20th century. Expansion of cultivated area, accounted only for one-half of this increase in output and therefore the other half came about through increased yields (Perkins, 1969: 37). The rise in yields could only be attributed to improved seeds, changing cropping patterns and new crops besides a continuous expansion and maintenance of water control besides development and application of new forms of fertilisers (mostly organic) (Ibid. Chapters 3 and 4).

4. Huang (1990): 12-13.

merely perpetuated the six centuries-old peasant economy, and though increases in yields were continually achieved, these were skimmed away by the Chinese state. Further, with no alternative productive employment for the 'surplus labour' in agriculture meant diminished returns per workday besides consumption levels persisting 'close to the margins of bare subsistence.'[5]

In Huang (1990), for the period 1950-1980, the analysis goes back and forth between two indicators of involution: (i) a stagnation of labour productivity (and when this does not support the hypothesis); (ii) a stagnation or decline in individual income.[6]

Empirical evidence however, on various aspects of the rural economy in general and indicators of production conditions in agriculture and related activities for the period since the 1960s, clearly displays an agrarian transition and a fundamental shift that is vastly different from the evolution in pervious epochs of China's agro-economic history. The rapid expansion of agricultural capital between 1965 and 1980 not merely expanded production possibilities, ensuring the building of a capacity to overcome the serious effects of the climatic disturbances that had plagued Chinese agriculture for centuries, but also made possible gradually increasing levels of consumption. The expansion in consumption within a framework of collective ownership of production accrued to the members of the communes, both as an economic as well as a social entitlement. This was possible by creation and expansion of employment both in direct agricultural production and indirectly in the creation of agricultural capital.

To view Chinese collectivist agriculture as a mere continuation on a six centuries-old 'involutionary' path by means of a single parameter namely productivity per unit of labour or its variant income per workday is a reductionism that fails to account for many other dimensions of the transformation that rural China underwent during the 30 odd years from 1950 onwards. The period from the early 1950s to the mid-1960s was one

5. Ibid.: 16.

6. 'There was an expansion in the absolute values of output and, to some extent, even in annual incomes per household, but this was due to more days worked by household members, especially the women, children and elderly, not greater net returns per day' Huang (1990): 306.

of experimentation with various forms of collective institutional arrangements in both agriculture and industry. A combination of factors such as a nascent administrative structure, extreme climatic disturbances, severe paucity of resources, underdeveloped transport and communications infrastructure, intense intra-Party political struggle, besides others proved disastrous for Chinese agriculture during the end of 1950s.

Rural Reforms in the 1960s and Expansion of Productive Capacity

By 1965, however, Chinese agriculture had largely recovered from the crisis of the late 1950s with changes in the organisation of production as well as larger support to agriculture from the industrial sector. Institutional reforms undertaken in the early 1960s, had put in place a structure more decentralised than the commune system.[7] Production teams that hierarchically functioned just below the communes became the new unit of accounting for purposes of production decisions, consumption needs and distribution of collective income.

Chinese official statements on pre-1978 policies especially with regard to the rural economy have been largely derisory. The 'Cultural Revolution' (1965-1975) in particular is viewed as a period of severe wide-ranging economic disruption. In recent years however, there appears to have been a moderation in the criticism of the overall political and economic strategy of that period, even in Chinese official documents. An officially sanctioned publication of 2006 notes that during 1965-1975, the performance of the agricultural sector was dynamic and that the impact of political interference on production was minimal.[8] The post 1965 development strategy that revolved around labour accumulation, the mobilisation of rural labour to carry out rural industrialisation and agricultural mechanisation and the extension of irrigation networks, was in effect a second attempt with the same strategy that had failed earlier. It was successful in the second attempt in widespread development of rural

7. 'Regulations on the work of the rural people's communes' introduced in 1962 laid down the operational mechanisms of the new structure. The functions of the production teams and below them the production brigades were significantly altered.

8. He (2006).

industry, expansion of irrigated area and ultimately enhancing rural living standards.[9] It has been argued that the collective structure of organisation made possible mobilisation of more 'surplus' labour for capital construction than might have been possible under private ownership and that there was a sharp increase in the already high figures of 1960s (Nickum, 1980). Financial support for agriculture took the form of a favourable, inter-sectoral terms of trade in the 1960s and the 1970s, besides large increases in direct state finance to agriculture and loans to communes that amounted to many times the value of tax collected (Ishikawa, 1981). (Figures 2.1 through 2.4 summarise the above discussion).

Figure 2.1

China: Investment in Agriculture, 1965-1979

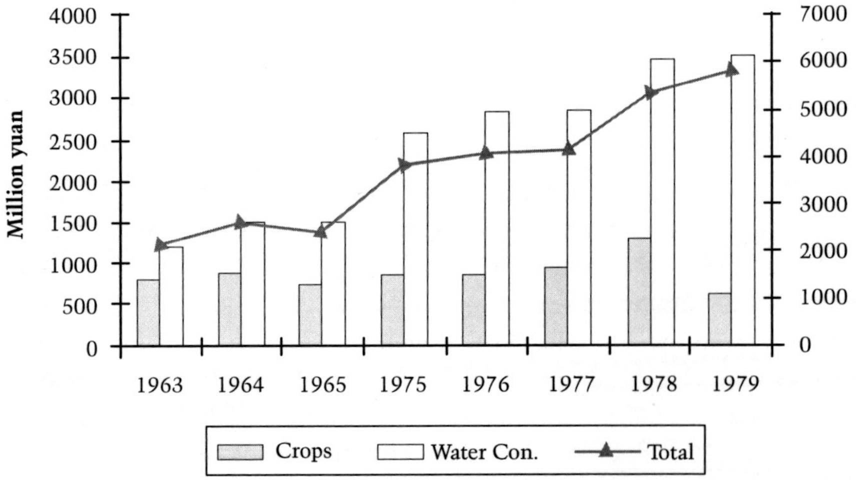

Note: Water cons. denotes all expenditure on water management in agriculture.

Source: *China Statistical Yearbook* (various years) and USDA (Agricultural statistical database for the PRC).

Compared to other Asian countries, China was able to achieve a greater labour absorption per hectare (especially in rice cultivation) along with higher yields per hectare of total agricultural production. This is attributed to the nature of technological changes during the period which

9. Bramall (2006) calls the revival following the calamitous 'Great Leap Forward' programme of the late 1950s, as 'late Maoist development strategy'.

Figure 2.2

China: Chemical Fertiliser Application, 1965-1979

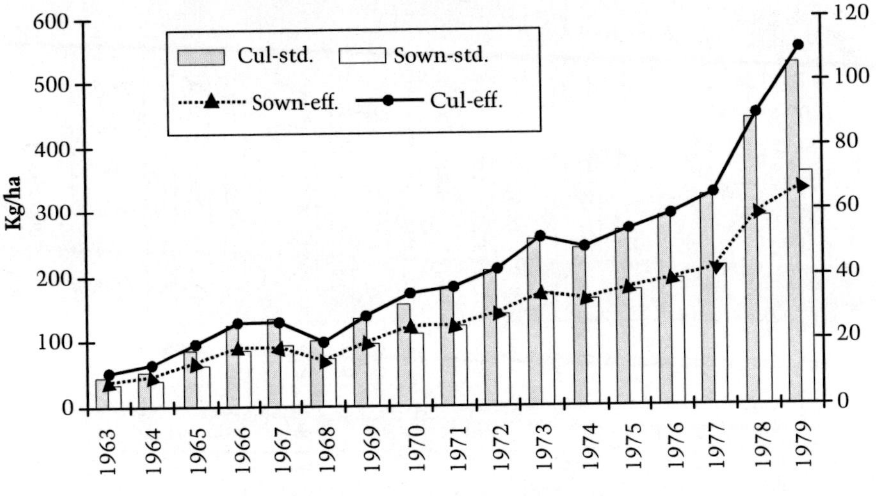

Note: Figures are in standard volumes and effective volumes per cultivated and per sown areas.

Source: *China Statistical Yearbook* (various years) and USDA (Agricultural Statistics Database for the PRC).

Figure 2.3

China: Agricultural Machinery, 1965-1979

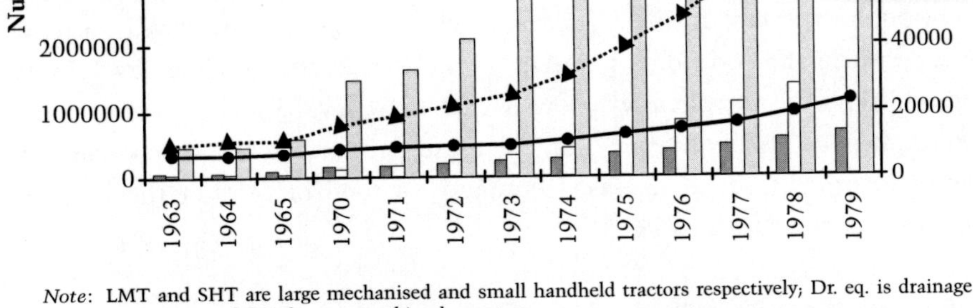

Note: LMT and SHT are large mechanised and small handheld tractors respectively; Dr. eq. is drainage equipment and CH denotes combine harvesters.

Source: *China Statistical Yearbook* (various years) and USDA (Aricultural Statisticsal Database for the PRC).

Figure 2.4

China: Sown Areas and Grain Output

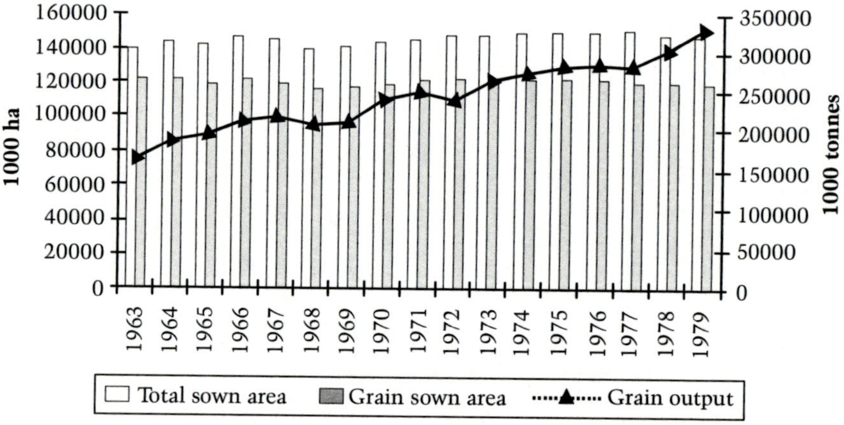

Source: *China Statistical Yearbook* (various years) and USDA (Agricultural statistical database for the PRC).

made it possible to increase the utilisation of the most scarce factor of production, namely cultivable land—land augmenting—as well as applying as much as possible, the abundant factor, namely labour. Hence labour use in order to increase total production (Ishikawa, 1982).

In the context of the above discussion on China's development strategy (and also applicable in general to most developing countries), Saith (1985) offers an illustrative framework that posits two basic conditions for balanced growth—employment balance (EB) and food balance (FB). Employment balance requires a growth rate that can absorb the net additions to the labour force. Food balance requires rates of growth of food that can feed the additional population, at least at the previous levels that are additionally not already below a threshold level to satisfy minimum requirements. This condition may be more demanding if increases in per capita incomes lead to increased demand for food i.e., either the income elasticity is constant or rising.[10]

10. In this model, the rates of growth of GDP and food output are determined given the dynamics of the growth of the labour force and the output-labour ratios. These rates are found to be high even to maintain both the balances at the minimum possible levels.

Comparing the experience of many developing countries within this illustrative framework three conclusions are drawn:

1. That only in exceptional cases are both the balances maintained.
2. In the majority of the cases, the experience with regard to overall growth has been better than that for the food sector—unbalanced growth, and
3. In the overwhelming number of cases, the food balance has been grossly violated.

Violation of the EB means a higher number of dependents per employed person and with rising per capita incomes implies an equitable sharing (of the restricted employment opportunities or) in unemployment. Within a socialist framework with universal entitlement to work, redistributive mechanisms operate to distribute available benefits of employment equitably between the employed and the unemployed, though slightly biased in favour of the former. When the FB is violated, again the equity principle operates. In a capitalist economy, however, imbalance with regard to EB leaves the unemployed without any means, unless social security mechanisms operate to alleviate the situation. A violation of the FB leads to a rise in food prices and given a skewed distribution of income, economic growth is conditioned upon the disentitlement to food or the creation of hunger.

The creation of hunger or disentitlement in the context of countries like China or India has been effected through changes in the composition of food produced and consumed, in the background of high growth that either occurs with an already skewed (as in India) or worsening distribution of income (China).[11] This is taken up in the following sections.

Rural Reforms and Agricultural Production since the 1980s

Institutional reforms in rural China had its origins in parts of eastern coastal provinces towards the end of the 1970s when households contracted with the higher administrative levels to meet targeted volumes of output. The officially sanctioned Household Responsibility System (HRS) in

11. See Patnaik (2007a and 2007b) for a detailed discussion of the Indian case.

agricultural production was introduced and developed in the early 1980s, it gradually embodied a broad perspective for the rural economy as a whole. The emphasis was on a comprehensive development of agriculture, industry and commerce. Substantial increases in procurement prices of agricultural output together with the release of labour consequent to the introduction of HRS created favourable conditions for diversification in the rural economy. The basic direction of the reforms was towards a progressive decentralisation of authority and responsibility and this gave rise to newer forms of organisations in agriculture, industry as well as commerce.

In the sequence of official reform policy changes, individuals were permitted to establish small businesses and trade in animal, vegetables and other minor products and also light manufactures like textiles and clothing in 1981. Correspondingly, the government removed many items from its procurement lists and in 1982, periodic markets began to grow rapidly in numbers and volume of goods traded. By the end of 1992, both the numbers of and volume of trade in rural markets grew exponentially and a national wholesale market for trade in grain was established besides several at the regional levels. Reforms in the rural economy continued through the 1990s, enabling rapid industrialisation of the countryside.[12] In a quasi-market framework especially with regard to the labour market, low wages along with substantial incentives for foreign direct investment enabled an explosion in the number and output of rural export-based industries (termed township and village enterprises, TVEs).[13] A large proportion of rural industries were concentrated in the eastern coastal provinces that attracted an unprecedented level of labour migration from less industrially developed rural areas and regions. An urban construction boom beginning in the mid-1990s additionally began to absorb large numbers of temporary

12. There is a large volume of literature on various aspects of rural reforms undertaken since the early 1980s until recent years. Ho *et al.* (2004) covers rural development under reforms; Rozelle and Summer (2003) examine Trade policy with regard to agriculture while Howe *et al.* (2003) elaborate discussions on reforms using official documents.

13. The erstwhile Commune and Brigade-run industrial and service establishments in rural China provided the foundation and transformed into TVEs during the initial burst of rural industrialisation. Sigurdson (1977) provides a comprehensive evaluation of the integrated rural industrialisation strategy of the late 1960s and the 1970s.

as well as permanent migrants from rural areas. Estimates of such 'floating labour' were in the range of 80-100 million during the mid-1990s and currently around 150-200 million.[14] A major landmark in the continuing reforms concerns the legal position of the use of agricultural land, the tenure of such use and also the rights of transferability. From an entitlement of 15 years as the period of household user rights for farmland in late 1990s, it was raised to 30 years in the early 2000s.

More recently, the 17th Party Congress (2008) coinciding with the 30th anniversary of 'reforms and opening up' revived the question of rural reforms in a major way, so as to map out the path for future development. Besides discussing issues of social security for rural residents and establishing a system of modern agriculture, the third plenary session approved the document 'Decision on Major Issues Concerning the Advancement of Rural Reform and Development'. Doubling farmers' income and eliminating absolute poverty by 2020 was one of the quantitative targets established. The 'decisions' that signal a fundamental institutional shift in agriculture, include calls for the development of special rural cooperatives in conjunction with formally recognising the farmers' rights to lease or transfer user rights besides establishing a system of rural insurance and enhancing agricultural futures markets.[15]

In agriculture, reforms have produced significant changes in cropping patterns in addition to a very high degree of diversification in farming and animal husbandry.[16]

The share of agriculture in GDP remained high at over 40 per cent in 1990 but rapidly fell to around 21 per cent by 2005 and within the broad agricultural sector, the share of farming fell from over 65 per cent to 50 per cent in the respective years (Figure 2.5).

---

14. It is important to note here that changes in the designation of rural towns and definitions of rural and urban areas beginning in the late 1980s, significantly altered the status of resident populations and also the interpretation for analytical purposes of the statistical data on rural and urban populations for the period until the mid to late 1990s are very complex.

15. For a detailed report on this document see China Quarterly (2009).

16. For a discussion of changes in output, labour absorption and employment in agriculture for the period up to the mid-1990s following reforms see Patnaik and Natrajan (2000).

Figure 2.5

China: Composition of Gross Value of Agricultural Output, 1990-2005 (Constant Prices)

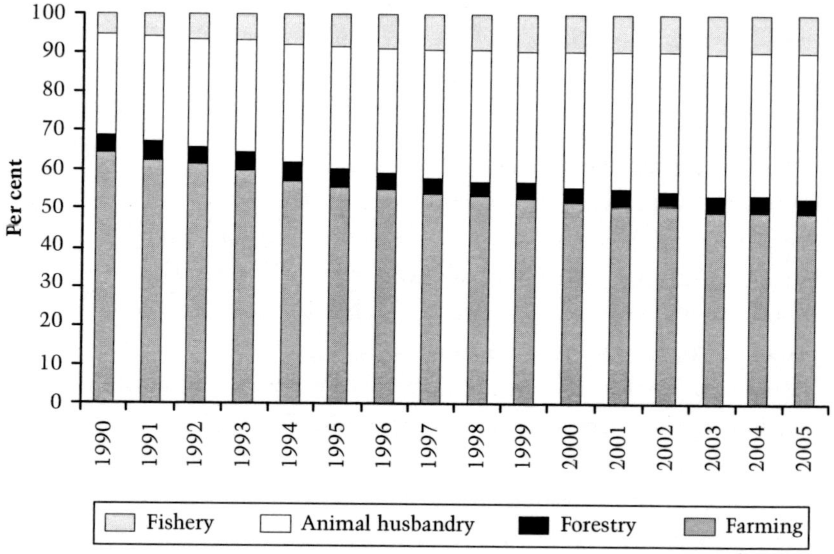

Source: *China Statistical Yearbook 2006*.

Figure 2.6

China: Sown Areas and Cereal Output, 1980-2007

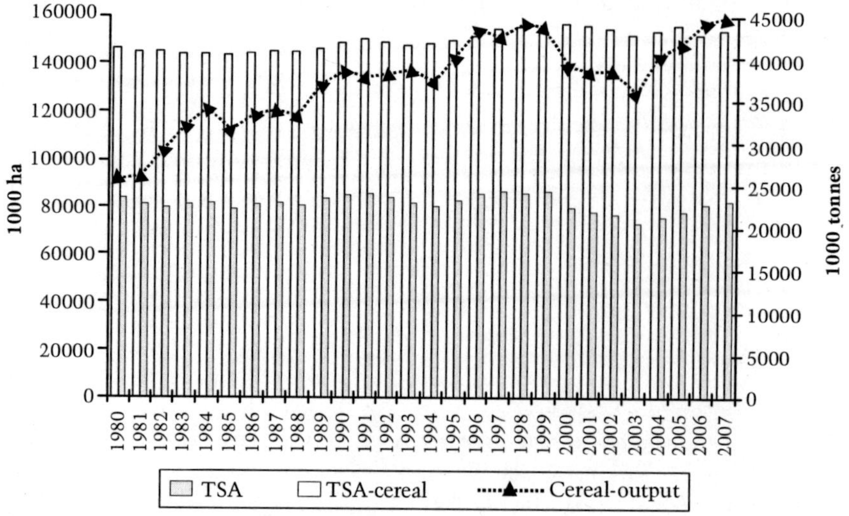

Source: *China Statistical Yearbook* (various years).

Total sown areas (TSA) recorded an upward shift since the mid-1990s, though the area devoted to grain crops, cereals in particular, has remained stable. Over the entire period 1980-2007, cereal output has followed long-term trends increasing slowly with regular drops owing to weather related factors (Figure 2.6). Since the early 1990s, the general trend with regard to non-cereal crops has been a significant increase in high value commercial food crops. In the case of major cereals,[17] output increase has been impressive—recording an over 70 per cent increase by 2006 over the volumes in 1980. This has largely been due to the increasing weight of maize in both the share in total area sown—from 14 per cent in 1980 to 19 per cent in 2007—as well as share of cereal output (see Figure 2.7). But the share of cereals (or grains by Chinese statistical definition that includes tubers—particularly potatoes—and soyabeans) in total area sown recorded consistent declines with a diversion of land towards high value food crops such as vegetables and fruits with increased shares (Figure 2.8).

Figure 2.7

China: Composition of Cereals Production, 1980-2007

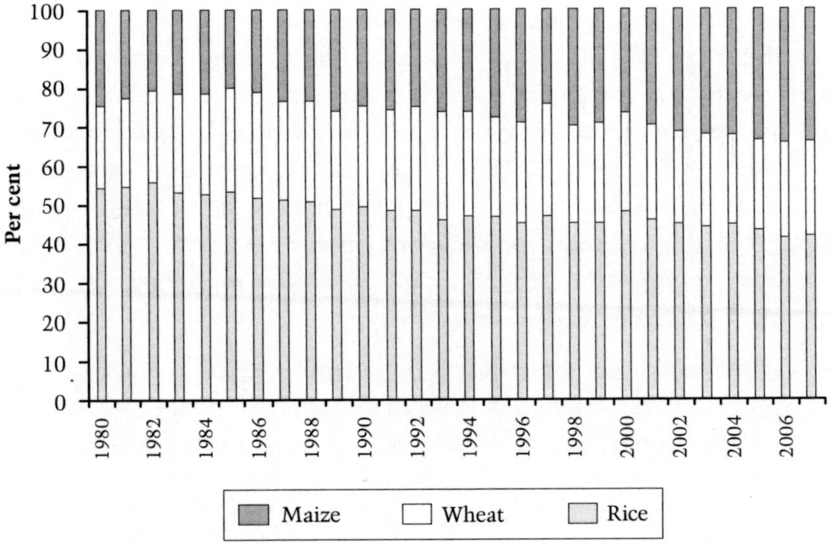

Source: *China Statistical Yearbook* (various years).

17. Here cereals include rice, wheat and maize only. Further, rice output in Chinese statistics is unhusked volume weight.

Figure 2.8

China: Sown Areas under Vegetables and Fruits, 1978-2007

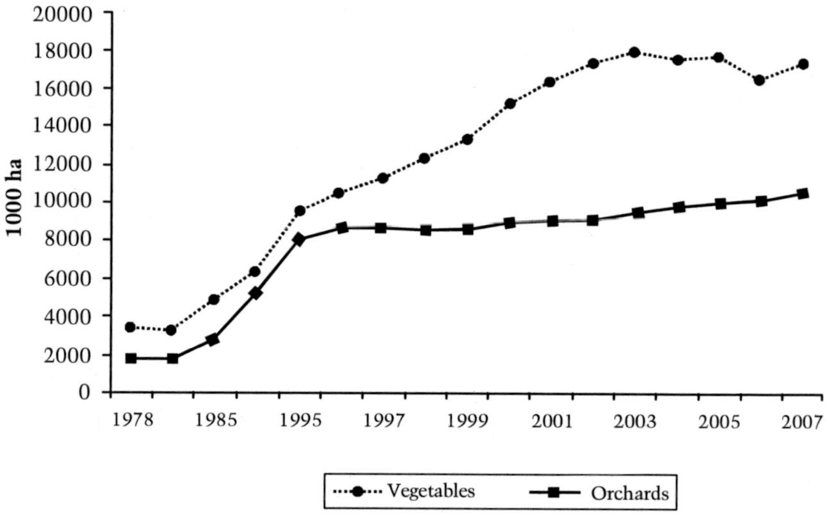

Source: *China Statistical Yearbook* (various years).

Besides these trends in farming, the major shift in food production since the early 1990s has been a steady rise in animal sources of food (poultry, dairy, aquatic and all forms of meat products). According to official statistics, per capita production of meat (includes pork, beef and mutton) rose from around 12 kg in 1990 to around 40 kg by 2007 and aquatic products from around 5 kg to 36 kg per capita in the respective years.[18] Grain production per capita on the other hand is reported to be around 380 kg in 2007 increasing from 327 kg in 1980. The peak, however, was in 1990 when the figure reached over 393 kg.[19]

For many reasons these figures do not provide an accurate picture of food availability per capita. For one, there are definitional problems that require careful interpretation, especially with regard to what is 'grain', or

18. Data from *China Statistical Yearbook 2007*: Table 12.21.

19. Ibid. Besides rice volumes estimated at their unhusked weight.
Official Chinese definition includes soyabean and potatoes besides rice volumes estimated at their unhusked weight.

the difference between husked and unhusked rice. Secondly and more importantly, what is produced is not exactly that available for consumption. Grain production figures per capita do not reveal the proportion diverted to external markets, or towards production of meat. For instance, the large increase in the output of corn in the past 15 years has largely been diverted as feed. While per capita figures of either production or availability indicate roughly the capacity of the system to feed the population, the more relevant parameter is changes in income distribution that determines the actual quantum of food that people in different income classes are entitled to. These issues are taken up in the next section where an alternative dataset prepared by the FAO is examined to reveal the dynamics of food consumption and composition in China since the 1980s.

Food Consumption and Composition in China since the 1980s

According to official Chinese reports, food consumption patterns in the past decade or more, have begun to resemble the beginnings of the 'prosperous' stage of economic development. With high levels of economic growth and increasing per capita incomes, official statistical representations frequently emphasise the decreasing share of food expenditures in total income—Engel's coefficient—to substantiate the claim of 'nutritional prosperity'.[20]

However, changes in consumption expenditure devoted to food or its proportion in total expenditure may not by itself prove to be a substantive indicator of a rise in basic standards of nutrition—or a 'prosperous' level of general food availability for two reasons:

1. The limited sample size of expenditure surveys from which official estimates of declining proportion of expenditure on food are derived

---

20. Ernst Engel's law states that as household income increases beyond a certain level, the share of food expenditure begins to fall, even though the absolute expenditure on food may increase. Just as for an individual, for a society too with increases in per capita GDP, Engel's law begins to operate and such a stage has been interpreted as the onset of 'prosperity' in official Chinese publications on this issue. For many years now, *China Statistical Yearbooks* and the provincial equivalents have included exclusive tables reporting the falling trends in the share of food expenditure in overall expenditure.

do not adequately represent actual consumption patterns as well as adequate food availability; and

2. Consumption expenditure surveys revealing higher average food consumption may be consistent with lower than prescribed norms of nutrition levels for the lower income classes, particularly with rising income inequality.

Further, in the case of China, published data on production and consumption of all categories of food do not seem consistent when examined closely by their respective components. In other words, the official claim of achievement in high nutritional standards in China is based on a growing per capita production of food grains, as well as on a continuous increase in the availability (production) of meat and meat products. Data from both the National Bureau of Statistics of China as well as FAO datasets are consistent in this regard. According to the latter source,[21] between 1990 and 2005, per capita meat (pork, poultry, beef and mutton together) availability more than doubled—from just over 25 kg to over 60 kg. Pork and poultry meat production accounted for most of the increase (see Figure 2.9).

But with regard to per capita availability of cereals (consumed directly as food) that accounts for a substantial proportion of calorie requirements, the trend has not been as impressive (see Figure 2.10).[22]

This contradicts the official pronouncement for the simple reason that the quantity produced is not identical with that available for direct consumption, and the official statements misrepresent production per

---

21. FAO's Supply Utilization Accounts (SUA) provide detailed data on production and domestic supply (availability) for every crop and food product where domestic supply includes net trade. Most work on China's food economy substitutes domestic production for availability as well as indicative of consumption. Under the SUA, domestic supply is not equal to consumption (as food). Utilisation of domestic supply takes the form of food manufacture, waste, feed and seed (where applicable) and other uses besides direct consumption as food. The discussion in this paper uses the term 'availability' not as a substitute for the technical FAO term 'domestic supply' but to the net amount or volume that is available as food or feed.

22. In fact, from the mid-1990s, there has been a gradual decline even though production per capita has followed an increasing trend (with declines in some years). It needs to be clarified here that the official figures for grain production per capita noted in the earlier Section varies considerably from those of the FAO reported in this Section due to different definitions. See *China Statistical Yearbook 2007*: Table 12.21.

Figure 2.9

China: Per Capita Availability of Various Meats, 1990-2005

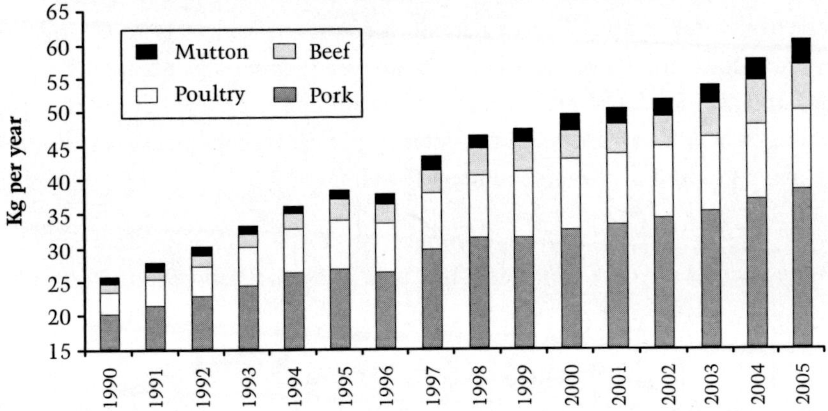

Source: FAO, Supply Utilization Accounts database.

Figure 2.10

China: Per Capita Availability of Major Cereals as Food, 1980-2005

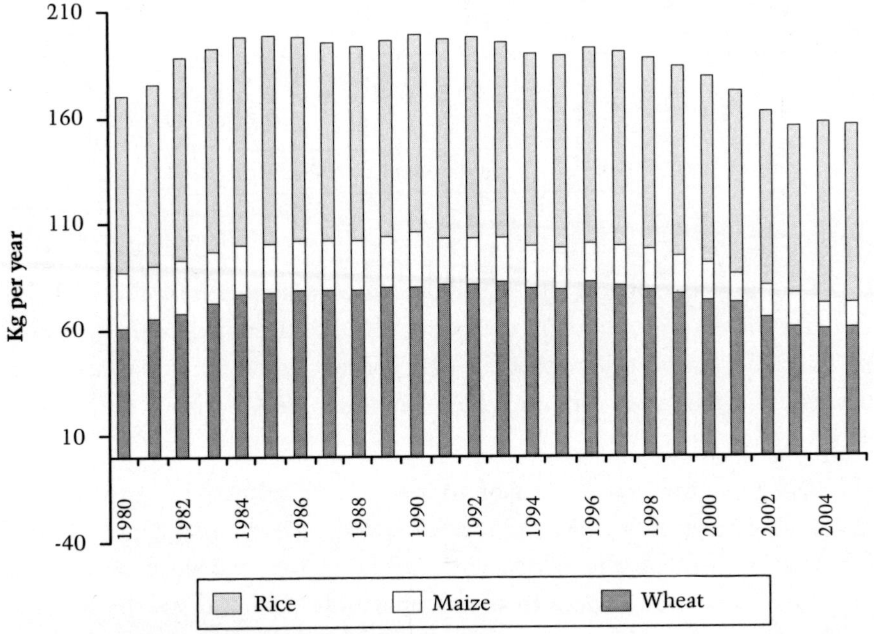

Source: FAO, Supply Utilization Accounts database.

capita as indicating consumption or availability per capita. This becomes clear when the figures for the total availability of cereals, by the proportions that are consumed directly as food, and indirectly as feed, are examined. While the total availability of cereals for consumption (as food and feed together) does not show significant increases as officially claimed between 1980 and 2005, the share as feed has gradually increased from the mid-1980s as a result of which the availability per capita for direct consumption displays a gradual decline (see Figure 2.11).

Figure 2.11

China: Availability Per Capita of All Cereals for Food and Feed, 1978-2005

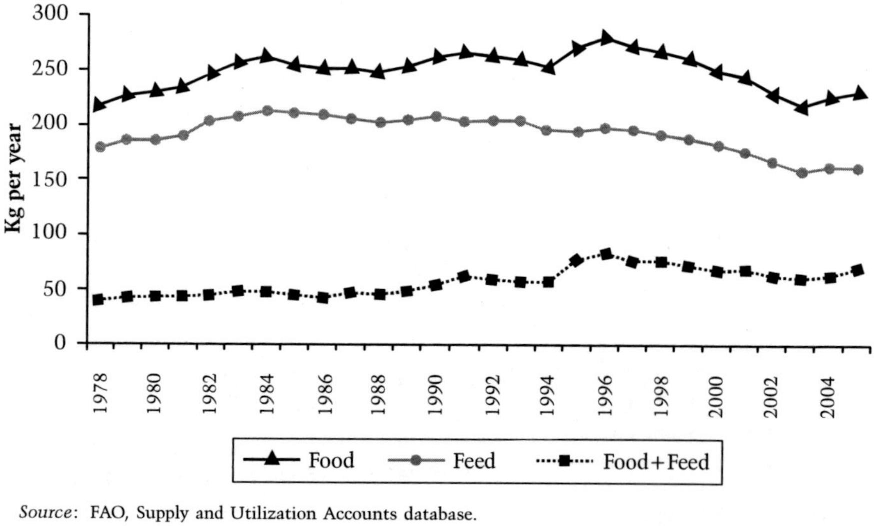

Source: FAO, Supply and Utilization Accounts database.

The large expansion in area allocated to maize cultivation and the resultant increase in output in the period 1980-2007 noted in the previous section needs to be understood in this context since maize began to be increasingly diverted as feed to achieve the high levels of meat output (see Figure 2.12).

Based on historical data of industrialised countries, and on the relationship between increasing incomes and changes in food consumption, it has been observed that along with falling shares of food expenditures (Engel's coefficient), changes in the composition of food takes the form of an increasing share of nutrition from animal sources. Per capita direct

Figure 2.12

China: Share of Maize in Cereals and as Feed, 1980-2005

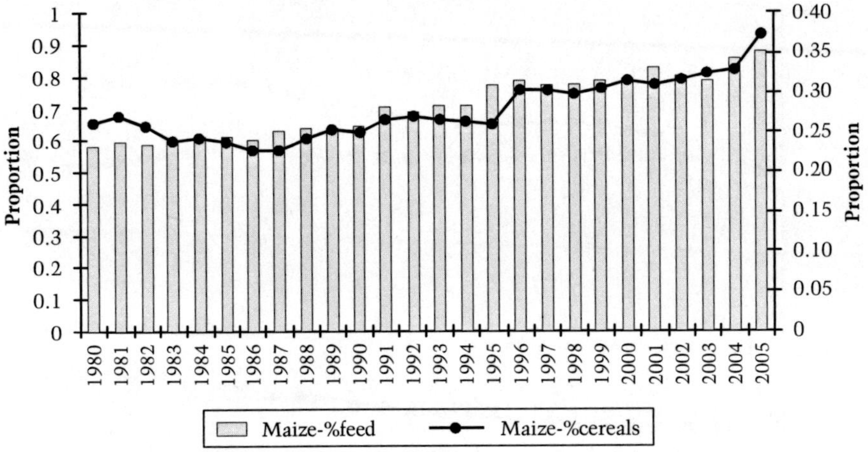

Source: FAO, Supply and Utilization Accounts database.

cereal (food grain) consumption levels continue to rise before beginning to stagnate or decrease while indirect consumption in the form of feed grains begin to increase (and soon surpass direct consumption) to provide for higher levels of nutrition in the form of protein and fat.[23]

At high rates of economic growth, increasing incomes are normally associated with a secular upward trend in the total consumption of grain (or cereals or vegetal matter in general for both direct and indirect consumption) displaying a secular upward movement. In the case of China however, since the mid-1990s, both the total availability of all cereals per capita as well as the availability for direct consumption began to gradually decline and an opposite trend in the case of indirect consumption levels per capita (see Figure 2.11). As regards overall nutritional levels—indicated by the total calorie availability per capita—the trend has been one of stagnation (see Figure 2.13).

That the challenge of food security in China is a serious one cannot be understated. When examined in the context of worsening distribution of income in all dimensions—inter-personal, inter-regional as well as rural-urban, the problem assumes greater significance for the economic and

23. Yotopoulos (1985) provides a basic theoretical model that elaborates this issue.

Figure 2.13

China: Sources of Per Capita Nutrition, 1978-2005

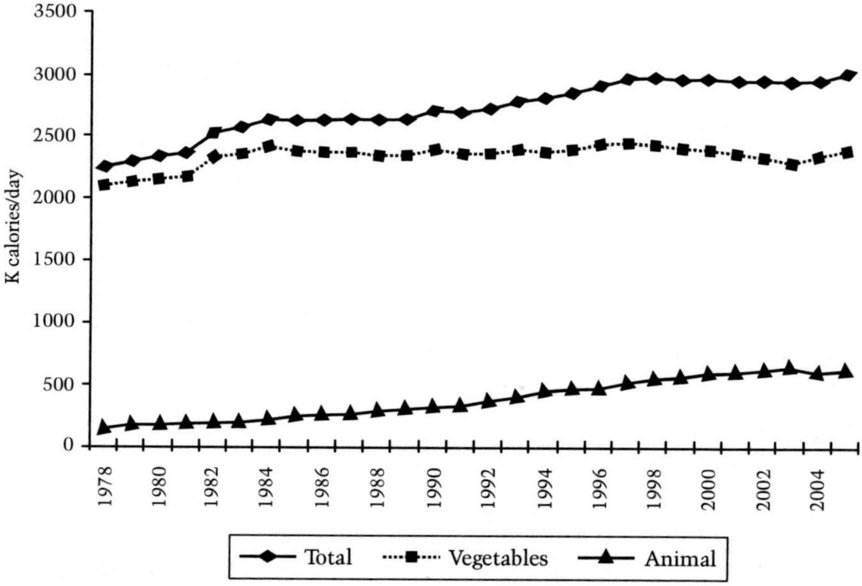

Source: FAO, Supply and Utilization Accounts database.

social sustainability of the current development strategy. Some of the issues that emerge from the discussion thus far are briefly discussed below.

Conclusion

By international comparisons, the trends in per capita nutritional levels in China since the 1990s have been fairly impressive. In 1990, total calories per capita in China surpassed the world average (at 2,700 kcal per day), and have remained above those levels ever since (3,000 kcal per day in 2005). This statistic is as significant as the reduction of population below poverty levels in China on a massive scale by the end of 1990s, that reduced global poverty.[24] Further, China's nutritional levels have been about 20 per cent higher in the past decade and a half in comparison to India

24. It must be noted here that official poverty threshold income levels have been fixed at a very low level and it is a very difficult and complex task to arrive at more reliable and representative figures.

where cultivated areas are 10-15 per cent higher. While average nutritional availability in China may be accepted as just about adequate by FAO standards, the real problem as regards food security is whether the availability translates into entitlement especially for the lower income deciles of the population.

In low-income countries, indirect demand for food (cereals) is a 'luxury'; animal protein (meat and animal products) are consumed mainly by high-income groups. As income levels rise, indirect demand for food grains by middle-income classes begin to expand. Under constraints of limited total grain availability, the competition for direct consumption by poorer groups and indirect consumption by middle and high-income groups intensifies. In China, high rates of growth since the 1990s has taken place within an institutional framework that has promoted concentration of wealth and income and in stark contrast to the pre-1978 period, income distribution has increasingly become skewed. The diversion of farmland towards high value food crops as well as towards production of feed grains is to be interpreted as a response to the demands arising out of the changing composition of food of higher income groups, rather than the official line that portrays these changes as signs of a movement towards a higher standard of nutrition for all sections of the population.

Most studies on income distribution in China (including official surveys and reports) have concurred on the widening disparities that have emerged in personal income. The Gini coefficient, which is derived from data on the shares of income that accrue to various income classes, grew from 0.33 in 1980 to 0.40 in 1994 and further to 0.46 in 2000. In 2005, this stood at a marginally lower level of 0.45 but above that of the USA at 0.41.[25]

Besides rising personal income disparities, the gap between urban and rural incomes over the last two decades has also continually widened. Recent data for 2006 shows that average urban income per capita was more than thrice the average rural income per capita. While urban incomes grew continually since the mid-1980s, average rural incomes stagnated or even

25. A Gini coefficient with a value of 0 represents perfectly equal distribution of income and of 100, a perfectly unequal one.

decreased between the mid-1980s and early 1990s. This trend re-emerged during the period 1995-2002, when rural incomes especially of those engaged in farming and agriculture stagnated. By 2003 when a modest 6.8 per cent higher income (adjusted for price increases) in farming income was recorded, average nutritional levels had already exhibited a decline. Rural per capita provincial variations in grain consumption were relatively low between 1995 and 2005 during which per capita consumption fell by 20 per cent[26] (sharing of hunger!).

As regards regional inequality, data on rural average per capita net income across the provinces reveal wide variations. Over the period until the mid-1980s, rural incomes grew fast following from policies that favoured agriculture and grain cultivation and the disparities across provinces were reduced considerably.[27]

China's participation in the international trade in grain and other agricultural products has, in recent years, vastly increased, and this requires further study in order to evaluate the future consequences of changing patterns of China's food and feed requirements. In 2004, 46 per cent (US $20.86 billion) of total trade surplus ($46.6 billion) was utilised for net agricultural imports (according to FAO trade data). Soya imports increased from 15 per cent of domestic supply (net available for domestic use) in 1995 to 68 per cent in 2005. In 2007, China's imports were equal to half of global trade in soya. While this saved China 13.3 million ha of farmland, in the exporting countries (Brazil, Argentina), it reduced the land for other crops.

Given the size of China's food requirements both current and future, the potential risks to food security in low-income developing countries that depend mainly on direct grain consumption to meet almost their entire nutritional requirements are immense.[28]

---

26. Estimates from *China Statistical Yearbook 2006*.

27. For a statistical appraisal of the evolution of rural inter-provincial income disparities see Natrajan (2006).

28. The potential risks therefore, to global stocks and supplies of grain due to production shortfalls in China combined with changes in food composition in favour of increased indirect grain consumption (via animal feed) are enormous (merely due to the scale of China's food demand—a 10 per cent shortfall in production or increase in demand translates to 25 per cent of global grain trade).

Notes:

i. *China Statistical Yearbook 2007* gives the proportion of cultivated area in total area at 13.54 per cent (130.04 million ha) where as the 1996 figures reports 9.89 per cent (94.97 million ha), 1995—9.94 per cent, 2004—at 130.04 million ha or 13.54 per cent.

ii. Data for the period 1965-1978 is compiled from various *China Statistical Yearbooks* and from the publicly available *Agricultural Statistics of the People's Republic of China* 1949-1993, of the USDA (United States Department of Agriculture), Economic Research Service.

References

Bramall, Chris (2006). "The Last of the Romantics? Maoist Economic Development in Retrospect", *China Quarterly* 187.

China Quarterly (2009). "Quarterly Chronicle and Documentation (October-December 2008)", *China Quarterly* 197: 236-82. March.

He, Kang (2006). *China's Township and Village Industries*. Beijing: Foreign Languages Press.

Ho, Peter, Jacob Eyferth and Eduard B. Vermeer (2004). *Rural Development in Transitional China: The New Agriculture*. London: Frank Cass.

Howe, Christopher, Y.Y. Kueh and Robert Ash (2003). *China's Economic Reform – A study with Documents*. London: Routledge Curzon.

Huang, Philip C.C. (1990). *The Peasant Family and Rural Development in the Yangzi Delta, 1350-1988*. Stanford: Stanford University Press.

Ishikawa, Shigeru (1981). *Essays on Technology, Employment and Institutions in Economic Development: Comparative Asian Experience*. Economic Research Series/Institute of Economic Research, Hitotsubashi University, Kinokuniya, Tokyo.

———. (1982). "Labour Absorption in China's Agriculture", in Shigeru Ishikawa, Saburo Yamamata and S. Hirashima (eds.), *Labour Absrortpion and Growth in Agriculture: China and Japan*. Geneva: International Labour Organisation.

Natrajan, Sriram (2006). "Inter-provincial Disparities in Rural 'People's Livelihood' in China: An Empirical Assessment (1980-2004)", *China Report* 42(3), August.

Nickum, J.E. (1980). "Local Water Management in the People's Republic of China", in Coward. E. Walter (ed.), *Irrigation and Agricultural Development in Asia*. Ithaca: Cornell University Press.

Patnaik, Utsa (2007a). "The Republic of Hunger", in U. Patnaik (ed.), *The Republic of Hunger and Other Essays*. Gurgaon, Haryana: Three Essays Collective.

———. (2007b). "Theorizing Food Security and Poverty in the Era of Economic Reforms", in U. Patnaik (ed.), *The Republic of Hunger and Other Essays*. Gurgaon, Haryana: Three Essays Collective.

Patnaik, Utsa and Sriram Natrajan (2000). "Output and Employment in Rural China – Some Post-Reform Problems", *Economic and Political Weekly* 35(38). September 16.

Perkins, Dwight H. (1969). *Agricultural Development in China 1368-1968*. Edinburgh: Edinburgh University Press.

Rozelle, Scott D. and Daniel A. Summer (2003). *Agricultural Trade and Policy in China: Issues, Analysis and Implications*. Aldershot, UK: Ashgate.

Saith, Ashwani (1985). "Primitive Accumulation, Agrarian Reform and Socialist Transitions: An Argument", *Journal of Development Studies* 22(1), October.

Sigurdson, Jon (1977). *Rural Industrialisation in China*. Cambridge, Mass: Harvard University Press.

Yotopoulos, P.A. (1985). "Middle-Income Classes and Food Crises: The "New" Food-Feed Competition", *Economic Development and Cultural Change* 33 (3).

3

Science and Technological Capability Building in China

Impact of Open Policies

V.P. Kharbanda

Introduction

The part played by the political 'structures' and 'superstructures', both in institutionalisation of modern science and technology (S&T), and in shaping its socioeconomic organisation, has been a dominant theme in the history of contemporary Chinese science (in the post war period). Historically, during the period up to 1985, the three national science conferences since 1949 held in 1956, 1962 and 1978 are viewed as key scientific events among the scientific community in China, which helped reform and re-mould the directions of institutionalisation and professionalisation of science and technology in China. The first plan period (1951-1956) was the period of rebuilding and reorganisation of scientific institutions through large scale import of technology from the then Soviet Union, and following the Soviet model of institution building with the perspective of 'Policy for Science' under dominant politico-bureaucratic culture. While the first two conferences were practically oriented towards building of technological capabilities in high technology areas in order to catch up with the advanced countries, particularly in regard to national defence, the 1978 conference was basically oriented to rebuilding and revitalising the scientific system in order to catch up with the advanced countries in the civilian S&T sector. This was to be done by adopting:

a) Open door policies for large scale foreign investments and import of technologies from the western world;

b) Revitalising and reorganising scientific institutions; and

c) Reviving the professional activities of the scientific community.

Thus pursuing the perspectives of 'Policy for Science' and the 'Science and Technology in Policy', simultaneously with the market-driven culture playing a crucial role for transfer of technologies, although again under the dominant politico-bureaucratic culture. In each of these conferences, the political leadership identified S&T as a major force of economic and social development and enthusiastically introduced new programmes with material support for institutionalisation and professionalisation of the scientific research system.

The 1985 reforms of the S&T system, further strengthened the above perspective of 'Science and Technology in Policy' and brought scientific institutions closer to the enterprises for commercial exploitation of indigeneous research through initiation of various programmes particularly in areas of high technology, creation of technology markets and development of S&T parks with market culture playing a predominant role under the dominant politico-bureaucratic culture. This paper discusses the efforts being made in China in terms of policies and programmes to build up and strengthen S&T capabilities for economic and social development in the post Mao era to meet the challenges of globalisation and international competition.

Chinese Science and Technology Policies and Programmes: Post Mao Era

The institutionalisation of the research and development (R&D) system and the basic infrastructure for S&T in China was accomplished in the 1950s and the early 1960s under the perspective of a 'Policy for Science'. However, the later periods between the years 1958-1960; and from 1965 to 1976 were disastrous for the growth and professionalisation of Chinese science, when all activities pertaining to basic research (except in few areas of high priority and defence research) and higher education could not be pursued under the ideology of the 'Great Leap Forward' and the Cultural Revolution. In the post Mao era, particularly after the 1978 S&T Conference, the S&T system was rehabilitated and revitalised under the leadership of Deng Xiaoping. By the early 1980s, the whole spectrum of the S&T system was infused with the norms and values of professionalisation of the scientific community (Kharbanda and Qureshi, 1987; Kharbanda, 1996; Gu, 2001). This restoration period entailed not only re-building of the S&T organisations but also building up of the new infrastructure for some crucial areas of S&T required in the coming decades. The debate on the new perspectives of market economy and liberalisation in technology acquisition, which began in late 1970s, pointed to the need for new changes from the mid-1980s (Yang *et al.*, 1997: 220-23). The system still lacked proper mechanisms for transfer of technologies from R&D institutions to the enterprises. A large number of research results achieved by the R&D labs could not find their ways into production (Gu, 2001: 213).

The Conference on 'Science and Technology Work' held in March 1985 was the watershed in the reforms of the Chinese S&T system, where science was considered as part of the production system. Premier Zhao Ziyang in his speech delivered to the Conference stated: 'Economic construction must rely on science and technology while scientific and technological work must be oriented to economic construction'. The ineffectiveness of the research system, lack of technology transfer from research institutions to production units and acute shortage of S&T manpower were major obstacles in achieving these objectives. It was proposed to solve these problems through opening of 'technology markets' for commercialisation of technical achievements by establishing close contact between research institutions and the enterprises. Use of economic levers and market regulations in the management of S&T were suggested to enable scientific institutions to develop internal impetus (Zhao, 1985: 1-7). The chief policy thrust was to introduce market mechanisms into the operation of the R&D system by reducing the government grants to put pressure on R&D institutes and creating technology markets for technology transactions between R&D institutes and industrial users (Gu, 2001: 212-13). Thus the policy measures were in the direction of reduced government financial support, establishment of a responsibility system and autonomy in R&D institutions and creation of 'technology markets' for effective transfer of technologies from research institutions to the enterprises.

The Third Session of the Sixth National People's Congress in April 1985 endorsed the proposals concerning S&T reforms, which called for further opening to the outside world for import of advanced technologies and revamping the existing S&T system to better serve the economic construction. Thus the perspective of 'Science and Technology in Policy' was in full vogue under the dominant market—industry self-reliant culture (Kharbanda, 1996: 145-46; Gu, 2001). To implement these reforms, a Chinese Patent Law was also enacted in April 1985 (Regulations), which was later revised in 1992 and again in 2003 in accordance with the WTO regulations. Conditions were created for setting up joint research institutions and enterprises. Government policies encouraged promising scientists to travel abroad for higher education and created favourable conditions for the return of overseas Chinese scientists. The government also allowed professionals to hold a second job in their respective fields (Kharbanda, 1996). During this period the policies that guided close interactions and merger between the research institutes and the industrial enterprises were also proposed and implemented.

In March 1986, the National High-Technology Research and Development Programme or the '863' programme was initiated for research in high technologies in order to acquire advanced technological capabilities in specific areas, combining excellence in research and commercialisation so as to reduce the technological gap with the developed countries (MoST, 1998; Feng, 2001: 13-14). A National Natural Science Foundation of China (NSFC) was also established in 1986 to give emphasis to basic research and applied basic research activities through peer review and excellence of the applicants.[1] In an attempt to strengthen scientific research and higher education, a series of measures were adopted like a 'Young Scientist Fund' set up in 1987, Special Fund for Middle-Aged and the Young Scientists set up in 1992.

In January 1987, the State Council promulgated the 'Law on Technology Contracts' which guaranteed the legitimate rights and interests of buyers, sellers and the intermediaries of technology.[2] The mandatory

1. The predecessor of the NSFC was the Science Fund initiated by the Chinese Academy of Sciences (CAS) from 1982, the first of its kind, to tap the country's scientific potential, discover and train scientific talent, and strengthen basic research (Beijing Review, 1982: 9). Its operational procedure was based on the National Science Foundation of USA.

2. To speed up the process of commercialisation of scientific research, the China Technology Market Management and Promotion Centre (Sinotechmart) was established in 1987 under the State Science and Technology Commission (SSTC). This promoted the development of 'science and technology parks', 'high technology industrial parks', and setting up of companies by research institutions, universities or by scientific personnel. A large number of 'spin-off' enterprises from R&D institutions under the CAS and the universities were the result of this policy.

planning mechanism was thus slowly replaced by a market-driven mechanism to mediate technology supply and demand between R&D institutions and the enterprises. A five-year schedule from 1986 to 1990 was also made to allow some 2,000 industrial technology research institutions[3] to become independent of the government support (Gu, 2001: 213).

In August 1988, a Torch programme (TP) to support and regulate new high technologies was also initiated by the State Science and Technology Commission (SSTC) with the objective of developing new and high-tech products in specific zones called high technology development zones (HTDZs), in close cooperation with universities and CAS research institutes.[4] This programme helps in commercialisation of high-tech and new technologies resulting from '863 programme' and 'National Key Technologies programme'. The Beijing New Technology Industrial Development Experimentary Zone, now known as the Zhongguancun Science Park was founded in 1988 and was the first of its kind in China and was based on the US Silicon valley.

> Since the first science park was created on the campus of Stanford University more than 40 years ago, Science Parks have been founded in many parts of the world. ...Zhongguancun is the name of a place in the Haidian district, northwest of Beijing, but currently the name connotes a high-tech Science Park similar to the Silicon Valley in the US (Wang, 2000: 1-2).

In 1999, it realised a trade revenue of 63.7 billion yuan and industrial output of 38.5 billion yuan. (Wang, 2000: 4). In 2000, it had more than 6,000 new and high-tech enterprises employing 50,000 people. Presently

---

3. These industrial technology research institutes include those which are affiliated to Central ministries and those affiliated to local industrial bureau at provincial and municipal levels. In 1993 there were 1,804 institutes under this group (Gu, 2001: 215).

4. A HTDZ is essentially a science and technology park (STP). This is equivalent to an industrial complex, close to a place of learning like universities, colleges or polytechnics or research laboratory having formal or informal links. It is designed to encourage formation of knowledge-based industries in a high quality and competitive environment. It has a management function for transfer of technology and business skills to enterprises on site; aims to reduce the time gap between scientific invention and its commercial application. The first STP was established in Stanford University, USA around 1950. However, the STP movement picked up only in late 1980s. At present there are 200 parks in the USA, 52 in UK, 86 in Germany, 27 technopolis in Japan, and 120 high-tech zones in China. In UK 52 parks have come together to form a Science Park Association (Naik, 1994).

there are 53 such national level zones. These house about 17,498 new/high technology enterprises. About 1,000 of them are affiliated with the educational sector. There are 670,000 researchers and engineers, 5,300 of them having PhD and 38,000 with masters degrees (Macdonald and Deng, 2004: 8-9). At present, China has 120 HTDZs at different levels. These zones have been developed with different specialities. For example, the 'Shenyang zone' features integration of machinery and electronics, while the 'Nanning zone' focusses on the development of agro-biotechnology. 'Daqing zone' established in 1992, places high priority on promotion and development of oil and petrochemical equipment and refined chemical technology. This zone enjoys cooperation from Qinghua University, Beijing, to develop low temperature nuclear heating systems to cope with severe winters. It has also linked itself with the Microorganism Research Institute of Chinese Academy of Sciences (CAS) in respect to a key project which relates to direct pouring of micro-organisms into the strata for raising oil recovery by 30 per cent. The first Torch belt was set up in 1991 in the Yangtze river delta with the approval of SSTC. In 1992, it undertook 120 Torch programme projects.[5]

The Torch programme had as its major thrust, the development of new technology enterprises (NTEs), which are basically spin-offs from R&D institutions.[6] Various forms of consortium among R&D and academic institutions and enterprises of various sizes, are also being encouraged. Multiple sources of funds have been opened up such as governmental 'leading funds', bank loans and foreign capital, in order to broaden the

5. The following description of the Torch Programme dating back to the mid-nineties is useful: Projects listed in the Torch Programme (TP) are entitled to secure funds from the State budget or preferential loans from banks for start-ups. Funding by the state increased from 750 million yuan in 1990 to 1.6 billion yuan in 1992. It is estimated that through the implementation of the TP, the total industrial output value may increase from 15 billion yuan in 1992 to 250 billion yuan by the end of the century. Out of the total of 12,000 projects, one-third are export-oriented (Wei, 1993: 18-23). The major technologies being developed in these zones relate to new materials, biotechnology, electronics, information, integration of machinery and electronics, efficient new energy sources, energy and environmental protection technology etc. Some high technologies, such as those in the fields of fibre-optic communications and electronic information have grown into major industries in Wuhan, Hubei and Beijing HTDZs (Beijing Review 1994, 37(18): 7).

6. This is supported by preferential tax treatment in the zones, special loans to finance new enterprises in fields such as biotechnology, high-energy physics, lasers, microelectronics, materials, computers and information technology, mechatronics, and ocean engineering.

resources for commercialisation of technology. Thus, a network of financing NTEs has been developed under the umbrella of decentralisation with three investors *viz.*, state-run R&D institutions, banks and HTDZs. While R&D institutions mainly provide venture capital for the initiation of NTEs, the banks provide fund for expansion of NTEs and HTDZs provide investments mainly for the development of the infrastructure. About 1,000 of NTEs, out of the total of 137,000, are affiliated with the educational sector. Most NTEs are located in urban areas with concentrations of R&D institutes and universities aiming at exploiting the potential of the available S&T expertise. For example Beijing and Shenyang have the highest concentration of NTEs (IDRC, 1997). The success of these NTEs has been widely accepted in China as they bridge the gap by creating innovative and autonomous NTEs (Gu, 1995; 2001: 37).

To further fortify basic research activities, a 'Climbing programme' was also initiated in 1991. By 1993, the SSTC and the Ministry of Foreign Trade and Economic Cooperation (MoFTEC) also granted decision-making powers in foreign trade to 100 scientific institutions to invest in R&D, production and marketing (MoST, 1993: 1). In 1998 to strengthen academia-enterprise linkages for innovative activities, a Knowledge Innovation Programme (KIP) was initiated, and is proposed to be completed by the year 2010. It is divided into three phases: (i) the initial phase was from 1998 to 2000; (ii) the implementation phase from 2001 to 2005; and (iii) the optimisation phase from 2006 to 2010. The KIP of CAS is a major component of the building up of the China's national innovation system.

By the mid-1990s, these market-driven policies had helped a number of industrial technology research institutions to move to the market place and became independent of the government.[7]

The National Science and Technology Conference held in May 1995, called for 'accelerating scientific and technological progress through the strategy of revitalising China through science and education' (Decision of the Central Committee of the Chinese Communist Party (CCCCP) 1995). It stressed 'stabilising one end and freeing up all the rest', which meant

7. In late 1995, the country's first 'University-Industry Cooperation Committee' (UICC) was established with the aim of accelerating the conversion of scientific research results into commercial products.

that one should maintain a small but highly trained research task force for basic, applied and high technology research and leave the rest some free play in the market. The main objective of this decision was to revitalise China through science and education, to implement fully the thought of S&T being the foremost productive force and regard education as the foundation, and to enable the economic construction driven by scientific and technological progress. It advocated that academic democracy should be truly practiced in S&T departments and the democratic spirit be rooted in the decision-making process for all major issues. Basic research should focus on finding solutions to the basic scientific theories and also technological problems in frontier disciplines, cross-disciplines and applied basic research. Collaborative research activities between research institutes, universities and enterprise should be promoted. The Scientific and technological resources of research and higher education institutions should be effectively utilised in the assessment, appraisal and assimilation of imported technologies. HTDZs to be promoted to nurture and develop high technology enterprises and in this regard, importance was to be given to a cluster approach.

Moving further in this direction, in 1996 the State Council issued the 'Decision on Deepening the S&T Reforms during the Ninth FYP (1995-2000) period', in which the emphasis was on developing high technologies and strengthening of basic research activities simultaneously (Li, 1996:1-21). Thus, knowledge generation and its exploitation through technological innovation became the prime objective. A need was also felt at this time that a national innovation system should be established to strengthen technological innovation activities. Policy decisions were taken to focus on basic research to emphasise basic theoretical and technological problems to face the future economic and social development. At the first plenary meeting of China National Science and Education Steering Panel held on 9 June 1998, it was agreed to establish China's National Innovation System (NIS) (Wang, 2004: 8). Strengthening collaboration between scientific research institutions and the universities in various forms (Zhu, 1999: 7-34) was also emphasised. In August 1999, China issued the 'Decision on Strengthening Technical Innovation, Developing High Technology, and Realizing Associated Industrialisation' (Jiang, 1999: 5; MoST, 2000: 10).

Finally, to bring excellence in scientific research and its immediate applications for industrial development, the National Conference on Technical Innovation on August 23, 2003 again called for the construction of a NIS. This was another milestone in S&T policymaking and reforms in China. In this framework, a programme for reviewing all public R&D institutes in the context of their potential for being a part of the NIS with enterprises as its mainstay has been taken up (Yuan Wang, 2004: 7-9). The component elements of the NIS are depicted in Figure 3.1 below:

China is putting special emphasis on the four pillars of this NIS with a network approach not only for absorption and adoption of imported

Figure 3.1

Actors of National Innovation System (NIS)

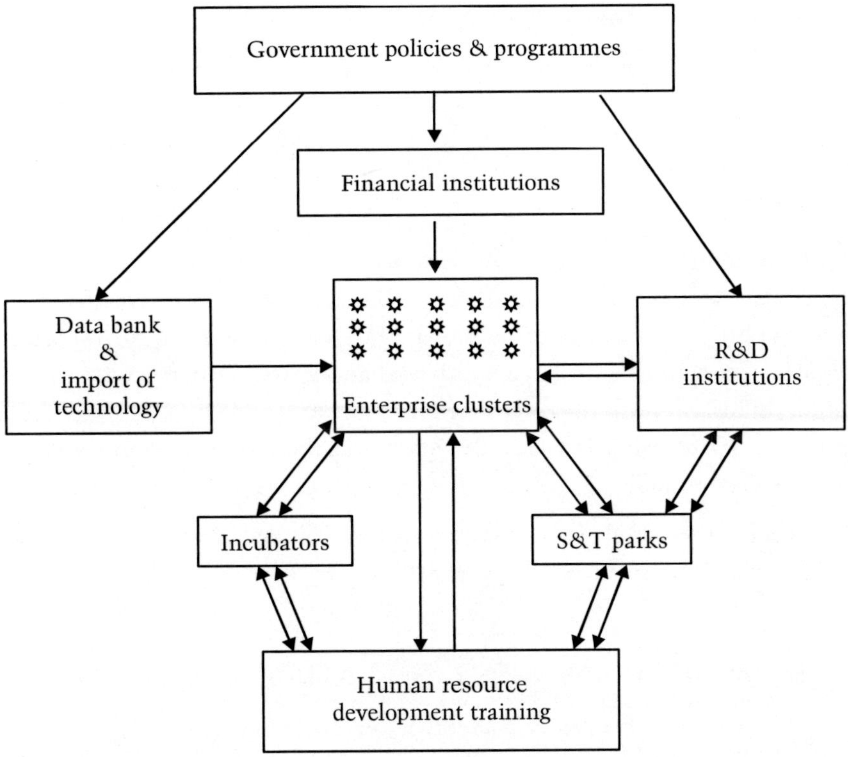

technologies, but also for creation of new technologies so as to be at the forefront of international competition. These pertain to:

- S&T human resource development.
- Promotion of R&D.
- Open policies.
- Venture capital.

Human Resource Development

In the aftermath of the Cultural Revolution, many Chinese observers noticed that there appeared to be a generation gap in Chinese science and technology. There were not many professional scientists who could take up leadership positions with the purpose of restoring professionalisation. Only a few middle-aged scientists were holding top positions (Suttmeier, 1977: 386). Premier Hua Guofeng admitted this in his speech at the Fifth National People's Congress held in March 1978.

> The gap between our own and the advanced world scientific and technical level which had been narrowing, has widened again in recent years. In all fields of endeavor, there are not enough trained young men and women ready to take over from older experts. The quality of school education has fallen sharply (Hua, 1978: 27).

In March 1978, the new leadership convened the National Science Conference, which was the third after 1956 and 1962 science conferences. About 6,000 S&T personnel participated. This was indeed an important national meeting, which revived the academic culture within the dominating framework of the Communist ideology, and thus commenced a new era of partnership between the State and the scientific community in the post Mao period.[8]

Accordingly, one of the main target of the seven-year science plan (1978-1985) to revive S&T system was to 'increase the number of

---

8. In 1978, Deng made an important speech at the National Science Conference convened by the Central Committee reiterating the lines proposed by Zhou Enlai in 1963. There was considerable alignment of thinking between Deng and Zhou Enlai.

professional and scientific researchers to 800,000'. Since then over the years major emphasis is being given on strengthening the S&T manpower resource which forms the foundation for any S&T activity to be taken. The growth of S&T manpower over the years is summed up in the following table. It will be seen that S&T manpower has increased considerably from only 0.425 million in 1952 to 5.276 million in 1980 to 28.48 million in 2002 (Table 3.1). The comparable picture regarding growth of S&T manpower in India is shown in Table 3.2.

Table 3.1

Stock of Scientific & Technical Personnel in China

(Thousand persons)

Year	*Engineering*	*Agriculture*	*Medicine*	*Scientific Research*	*Education (Teaching)*	*Total*
1952	164	15	126	8	112	425
1978	1571	294	1276	310	894	4345
1980	1862	311	1530	323	1250	5276
1985	3404	451	2161	336	1465	7817
1990	5101	551	2720	291	2146	10809
1995	5626	536	3035	303	9634	19134
1996	5745	579	3131	303	10162	19920
1997	5681	611	3214	302	10648	20455
1998	5719	636	3255	291	11075	20976
1999	5655	654	3330	284	11508	21431
2000	5551	670	3372	275	11783	21651
2001	NA	NA	NA	NA	NA	21698
2002	NA	NA	NA	NA	NA	28480

Source: SSTC (1993). *China S&T Indicators 1992*. Beijing. (In Chinese); SSTC (1998). *Science and Technology Statistics-Data Book,1997*. Beijing, p.47; and *Science and Technology Statistics-Data Book, 2001*. Beijing; MoST, p.40. *http://edu.cn.*(Ist January 2001); *China Facts and Figures* (2003), Beijing: New Star Publications. p.120. State Council Information Office (2003). *China in Diagrams*. Beijing: China Intercontinental Press. p.199.

Table 3.2

Growth of the Total Scientific and Technical Manpower in India: 1950-2000

(Thousand persons)

S. No.	Category of Personnel	Stock							
		1950	1955	1960	1965	1970	1980	1991	2000
1	Engineering degree holders	21.6	37.5	62.2	106.7	185.4	221.4	546.7	969.5
2	Engineering diploma holders	31.5	46.8	75.0	138.9	244.4	329.4	873.9	1456.0
3	Science post-graduates	16.0	28.0	47.7	85.7	139.2	217.5	482.0	767.1
4	Science degree holders	60.0	102.9	165.6	261.5	420.0	750.5	2430.3	3837.7
5	Agriculture post-graduates	1.0	2.0	3.7	7.7	13.5	96.5@	168.4@	231.2@
6	Agriculture degree holders	6.9	11.5	20.2	39.4	47.2	-	-	-
7	Medicine degree holders	18.0	29.0	41.6	60.6	97.8	165.4	310.3	403.4
	Total	155.0	257.7	416.0	700.5	1147.5	1780.7	4811.6	7664.9

Source: Department of Science and Technology (1999 and 2002). @ including graduates.

The above two tables clearly show that the growth of S&T manpower over the years in China has been higher than in India.

Promotion of R&D

The fact that since 1997 there has also been an increasing global trend of shifting most of the R&D activities of the Multinational Companies (MNCs) to the developing countries, particularly India and China, indicates that these countries have acquired enough R&D skills and capabilities in terms of scientific and technical manpower, and the low cost of research activity. In China, in November 2001, on the eve of China's WTO accession, the Nestle Group launched its first R&D centre in China.

Thereafter, a large number of MNCs notably Microsoft, IBM, General Motors, Lucent Technologies, Intel, DuPont, Proctor & Gamble, Nokia, Siemens, and Panasonic have set over 100 R&D centres in China, focussing on computer science, communications, automobiles and pharmaceuticals (Tang, 2003: 24).

In assessing the number of R&D centres set up in China by the MNCs, one has to take into account the ambiguity about defining 'R&D centres'. According to online *China Daily* there were 400 R&D centres set up by 400 corporations, out of the 500 MNCs operating in China (Most World Top 2003). Yet another recent paper by Zedtwitz has reported 199 R&D centres set up by MNCs (Zedtwitz, 2004: 440). However, according to Mani (2002), the share of R&D expenditure of the foreign R&D centres in the total industrial R&D expenditure is insignificant both in India and China. Further, R&D is directed to customising products for local market conditions. In practice, R&D moves very slow as compared to production, sourcing and other business activities. There has also been enhanced R&D activity on the part of the private and public enterprises in both the countries. In India around 1,180 R&D centres have been established by private industries. In China, in one region alone there are 500 R&D centres including 45 previously established centres by MNCs. This enhanced capability in research is also shown by the increase in number of patents filed by enterprises in India and China respectively in the US Patent and Trademark Office (USPTO), as shown above in the previous section. In this, the share of patents filed by the MNCs is considerable for both the countries. Out of the total patents filed from India by the top 50 assignees, the share of MNCs was 45 per cent, while the rest 55 per cent were held by Indian public and private organisations. In the case of China, it was 26.6 per cent and 74 per cent respectively (Mahmood and Singh, 2003: 1051-52). In recent years, China's R&D expenditure has increased more than 10 times from US $3.45 billion in 1995 to more than US $38.01 billion in 2006 (Table 3.3). In case of India, the respective figures for the same years are US $1.55 billion in 1995 to only US $6.62 billion in 2006 (Table 3.4). In this the share of the government, industry and others was 24.7 per cent, 69.1 per cent and 6.2 per cent respectively. However, industry provides most of its R&D funding through their own R&D activities (Chang and Shih, 2004). In case of India, the expenditure by private industry is still very low (23 per cent).

Table 3.3

Total Expenditure on R&D in China, 1980-2006

(¥ Billion)

	Yuan	*US $*	*% of GNP*
1958	.298	-	-
1965	2.717	-	-
1970	2.996	-	-
1980	5.332	3.58	1.5
1985	8.383	2.85	-
1990	12.543	2.65	0.71
1995	28.6	3.45	0.50
1998	50.11	6.60	0.69
2000	89.60	10.70	1.01
2001	104.25	12.59	1.09
2002	128.76	15.53	1.1
2003	153.96	18.57	1.13
2004	196.63	23.77	1.23
2005	245.0	29.62	1.33
2006	300.3	38.01	1.42

Sources: Various issues of *Beijing Review, China Daily* and *China Science and Technology Newsletter*.

Table 3.4

Total Expenditure on R&D in India, 1948/49-2005/06

(Rs. Billion)

Year	*Rupees*	*US $*	*As % of GNP*
1948-49	0.011	-	-
1965-66	0.684	-	-
1970-71	1.396	-	-
1975-76	3.567	-	-
1980-81	7.61	0.89	0.58
1985-86	20.69	1.38	0.83
1990-91	39.74	2.28	0.79
1995-96	74.84	1.55	0.71
1999-00	150.90	2.56	0.87
2000-01	178.12	3.68	0.94
2002-03	180.88	3.89	0.81
2003-04	197.26	4.29	0.78
2005-06	287.76	6.62	0.89

Source: Department of Science and Technology (2002; 2004; 2008).

Open Policies

Foreign Direct Investments and Role of MNCs

Technology is a critical input in the industrialisation and development. One of the most important means of technology transfer has been the foreign direct investments (FDI) by the MNCs in developing countries. With more liberal economic policies adopted by developing countries, this process of investment involving, technology transfer has been viewed as the easiest way of getting advanced technologies. With globalisation, access to foreign technologies has been liberalised, and as a consequence FDI in the newly industrialising countries like Korea, Taiwan, Singapore and Hong Kong, and emerging economies like India and China is on the increase. While in India, FDI increased from about US $1 billion in 1991, to only about US $3.5 billion in the year 2002 and to US $22.95 in 2007. In China it increased rapidly from US $25.5 billion to US $52.7 billion and US $83.52 during the same period (Table 3.5). In a way, this has enabled China to acquire advanced technologies, which is linked to export performance relating to high technology goods (Table 3.6). However, many of the public enterprises are lagging behind in this process of technological modernisation which indicates that the import of advanced technologies is not being coupled with the indigeneous R&D system to acquire technological capability. In India too, enterprises are not backed up with sufficient R&D for import of technologies which lead to repetitive imports of technologies (Kharbanda, 1993; Sandhya and Jain, 2003). The Indian experience also shows that FDI has not been helpful in raising the indigeneous technological capability of the enterprises. This is also seen in the fact that while the share of developing countries as recipients of FDI went up, their share in global technology transfer has been going down (Kumar, 1998; Mani, 2002: 21). It is also seen that more than half of the export growth in China is led by the MNCs (Susan, 2003; Gilboy, 2004: 35-36). The presence of MNCs in developing countries contributes mainly to export activity which is driven by cheap labour, but indigeneous technologies content (Lall, 1998: 46). Even though China has adopted a robust approach to attracting FDI, to what extent this is related to improving indigeneous technological capability and dynamism needs to be further explored.

Table 3.5

Foreign Direct Investments (FDI) Inflows in India and China, 1991-2007

(US $ billion)

Country/Year	*1991-1996 (Average)*	*1997*	*2000*	*2002*	*2005*	*2007*
India	1.085	3.619	2.319	3.449	7.61	22.95
China	25.476	44.237	40.772	52.700	72.41	83.52
Asia	59.411	109.092	142.091	94.989	165.00	319
World	254.326	481.911	1392.957	651.200	916.28	1833

Table 3.6

National Imports and Exports of High Technology Products (2001-2006)

(US $ billion)

Year	*2001*	*2002*	*2003*	*2004*	*2005*	*2006*
Exports	46.45	67.86	110.32	165.36	218.25	281.45
% of total exports	17.5	20.8	25.2	27.9	28.6	29.0
Imports	64.11	87.84	119.30	161.34	197.71	247.30
% of total imports	26.3	28.1	28.9	28.7	30.0	31.2

Source: China Science and Technology Data Book 2007.

Venture Capital

Venture capital in China represents a set of major institutional changes especially after the shift from the central planning system operating in early 1980s to the market reforms initiated in 1984. The system that emerged in the 1990s consisted of three primary institutional actors. First, R&D institutes and universities played the primary role at the start-up stage, providing both the original technology and the seed capital for the venture. (Gu, 1999: 82-84). The next set of actors were the banks, who were the primary source of financing. Although representing only 10 per cent of the investment in 1988, when the Torch programme began, their share increased to 50 per cent by 1990 and to 70 per cent in 1991. The third source was the complex of HTDZ, which provided physical space and funds for infrastructure facilities.

However, by mid-1990s, the government realised the shortcomings of this system for establishing new ventures to pursue broader national development objectives. This was due to three factors: first, the initial seed capital was too small; second, banks were in crisis due to non-performing loans; and third, the Central or the local governments did not have the surplus funds to step in as alternative financers for new ventures. Although, the China New Technology Venture Investment Corporation was established in 1986, it operated as a state-owned enterprise (SoE). Thus as any other SOE in China it was not profit oriented (White *et al.*, 2002: 6).

Gradually from 1995, the perception of venture capital shifted from its being a type of government funding to being a commercial activity to support new technology ventures. The founding of the domestic venture capital firms (VCFs) began with the establishment of local government funded venture capital firms (GVCFs), followed by university-backed venture capital firms (UVCFs). With the decision at the Ninth Conference of the National People's Congress in 1998, corporate-backed venture capital firms were also established and with this, there was a wave of VCFs involving government, corporate and foreign capital. Over the years thus, now four types of VCFs have evolved which pertain to government, corporate, university and foreign-backed, as the primary agents to finance new ventures in China. VCFs at present are the primary source of funds for new technology ventures and as of 2002, there were 210 VCFs operating in China. Of these foreign funded VCFs have become the major source (Ibid.).

These organisational changes and initiation of programmes for commercialisation of research results in China have brought research institutions and the enterprises into a close symbiotic relationships and linkages (Kharbanda, 1999; 2000) during the last decade, which are discussed as under.

University, Research and Industry Relations

In China, up to 1985, close academia-industry interactions were almost non-existent (Gu, 2001: 212-14). The S&T reforms initiated in 1985 were directed to intensifying such a relationship. Since there has been significant progress in linking research institutes with production, which has facilitated efficient technology transfer through various measures. The country's first university-industry cooperation committee was established in October 1995 to accelerate the translation of scientific results into commercial products. Accordingly, Qinghua University, a renowned institution and 38 large and medium industries entered into collaborations under the auspices of the Committee. The major partners were Baoshan Iron and Steel Complex at Shanghai, Guangdong Nuclear Power Corporation, Huaneng Corporation at Beijing etc. (MoST, 1995: 4). Over the years, following mechanisms have been evolved for closer linkages between R&D institutions, academia and the enterprises. These are as under:

Contract Research

In 1985 alone, 7,469 technology transfer contracts were signed by academic institutions with industrial or other recipients. Classified by category of recipients, large and medium sized state-owned enterprises accounted for 47.9 per cent, small state-owned enterprises for 29 per cent, collective enterprises for 7.4 per cent, village and township enterprises for 9.6 per cent and other entities for 6.1 per cent (Huang, 1988: 18). Statistics revealed that about 80,000 S&T research projects were being conducted in China's more than 1,000 institutes of higher learning by 1993. An investigation of 17 colleges and universities in Beijing, Shanghai, Jiangsu and Hubei showed that during 1991-92, more than 5,000 inventions by college students have been put to use (Beijing Review, 1993: 21-23)

Teaching-Research-Production (TRP) Associations

For university-industry cooperation, a number of 'TRP associations' have also been formed. These associations help in facilitating transfer of technology for new products and processes developed by the academic institutions to small and medium sized or village and township enterprises, as they lack R&D capability. University cooperation with large and medium sized enterprises is also growing steadily. This is intended to help: a) update their technologies; and b) assimilate the newly introduced foreign technologies. A number of universities in China are shifting to manufacturing in order to finance their research and educational programmes. For example, Beijing University has established a number of companies e.g., the Beida New Technology Company; the Beida Fang Zheng Company and Beida Weiming Bio-engineering Company (Cui, 1993: 19-22). According to reports, per capita R&D expenditure by these university-run enterprises was about US $850 in 1995 (China Science, 1995: 3-4), which is much higher than the average per capita expenditure on R&D in China. The success of these college-run enterprises set up by the universities is evident from the fact that some of them have been listed among the country's top 100 high-tech enterprises. These are Beijing University's Founder Group, Xi'an Jiaotong University's Kaiyuan Group, Qinghua University's Ziguang Group and Fudan University's Fuhua Group (China Daily, 1996: 4).

High/New Technologies Pioneer Service Centres (PSCs)

These PSCs (also known as incubators) have been established in high-tech zones to transfer scientific research results to production. The first such centre was founded in Wuhan in Central China in 1987. Since then, more than 70 incubators have been established in various provinces and cities. These centres provide researchers a place to turn scientific results into technical applications. These thus act as 'incubators' for research institutes and enterprises. Firms and research institutes only have to pay low rents to develop their products. These products are exempted from tax for a period of two years. It is claimed that PSCs in various provinces and cities have become an important part of the Torch programme to the extent that the Shanghai Scientific and Technical Innovation Centre has set up a 'Pioneer village' where all institutions of higher education and research are entitled to enjoy preferential policies granted by the state. Services such as industrial and commercial registration for enterprises, housing lease and facilities for loan are available (Wei, 1993: 18-23).

Joint Exhibitions

Another important form of linkage is the holding of joint exhibitions by academia and industry. One such exhibition was co-sponsored by the Central Committee of the Chinese Communist Youth League (CCCCYL), the All-China Students Federation (ACSF) and the Sida Technology Development Centre—a non-governmental corporation in Beijing. The 470 items on display were selected from 5,000 inventions submitted by 600 Chinese colleges in a national-level contest for student inventions in various fields like machinery, electronics, chemicals, computer sciences and telecommunications. Nearly 1,000 industrial units entered into negotiations for technology transfers. Of the prize entries, eight were put up for auction. For example, the ultra-fine magnetic production technology invented by Gu Hongchen and two other students from East China Chemical Engineering College earned the top bid of more than two million yuan and was bought by Shanghai Printing Ink Factory. According to experts, bio-adhesives developed by students at Jilin University are at par with advanced international standards. Organisers of the exhibition felt that institutions should track markets and economic development and adjust curriculum accordingly (Beijing Review, 1993: 21-23). To promote such relationships, China has established its first University-Industry Cooperation Committee to accelerate the translation of scientific research results into commercial products. In this direction, law on Transformation of S&T Achievements was also enacted (MoST, 1995: 4).

Research Output

Publication of scientific journals and research papers was resumed after the Cultural Revolution with the revival of the academic research and publication activities contributing to generation of knowledge. Since 1980, after the Cultural Revolution, there has been a continuous increase in the publication of research papers in China. There has been a spurt of knowledge generation activities, through increased publications of journals (Table 3.7; Figure 3.2). India in contrast presents a, picture of stagnation. China now publishes many more scientific journals than India. According to Ren *et al.* (1999: 1683), there are about 4,294 scientific journals[9] in China in 1999, while India had almost half of this i.e., 2,255 in the year 2000. This is due to the fact that every university, institute and professional society in China has at least one and in many cases, more than one publication. However, many of these journals seem to be of low international quality; as a result, Chinese journals are lagging behind those in rest of the world. This is shown by the fact that the number of Chinese scientific journals covered by Institute of Scientific Information (ISI), Philadelphia has been decreasing over the last 15 years. Analysing the Chinese physics and chemistry journals, Ren and Rousseau (2002: 389-405) conclude their low international visibility. As shown by Science

9. According to Baark there were 5,000 S&T journals in China during early 1980s. (Baark, 1982: 4).

Citation Index (SCI) of ISI, while there has been increase in the research papers published by Chinese scientists from 3,475 in 1983 to 14,610 in 1998, the per cent of papers published in Chinese domestic journals has decreased from 43.2 per cent to 17 per cent. Further, the highest impact factor (IF) for the Chinese journals was also very low in 1999, which was 0.5 (Ren *et al.*, 1999: 1683). At the international level India also faces a somewhat similar problem as China.[10] There is urgent need for concerted efforts to improve the quality of scientific journals in both countries through a system of vigorous peer review and referral. However, China has improved its international standing considerably since 2003[11] (China's 5th

Table 3.7

Output in Science and Technology Papers by Discipline in Domestic Journals in China (1991-2000)

(Number)

Discipline/ Year	*1991*	*1992*	*1993*	*1994*	*1995*	*1996*	*1997*	*1998*	*1999*	*2000*
Basic disciplines	23941	26320	27051	28566	27700	30048	33052	32300	34875	38385
Medical sciences and health	17042	18040	19198	20504	20464	23422	24472	29635	40735	45257
Agriculture, forestry, animal husbandry and fisheries	11663	11235	11345	10830	9557	9125	9366	9636	11923	13609
Industrial technology	41789	42980	44389	47592	50270	53644	53961	61770	75246	83597
Total	94435	98575	101983	107492	107991	116239	120851	133341	162779	180848

Source: Data on the basis of Ministry of Science and Technology of PRC (2000): 62-63.

10. A series of articles on the quality of Indian science emerged over the last few years particularly in issues of *Current Science* highlighting this problem. See for example: Sen and Lakshmi (1992); Ramaseshan (1992); Raghuram and Madhavi (1997); Virk (2000); Jain (2000); Vohora *et al*. (2001); Mariappan and Balasundaram (2002); Gupta (2002); Arunachalam (2002); Balaram (2002); Chopra (2004). The IF of Indian journals is also very low. The highest IF was that of *Current Science*, 0567 in 2000 (Jain, 2000: 1513).

11. In 2002, the number of research papers authored by Chinese scientists in SCI further increased to 40,758, advancing its position from 20th in 1985 to the 6th place in the world, after US, Japan, UK, Germany and France.

Figure 3.2

Output of Science and Technology Papers in China(1991-2000)

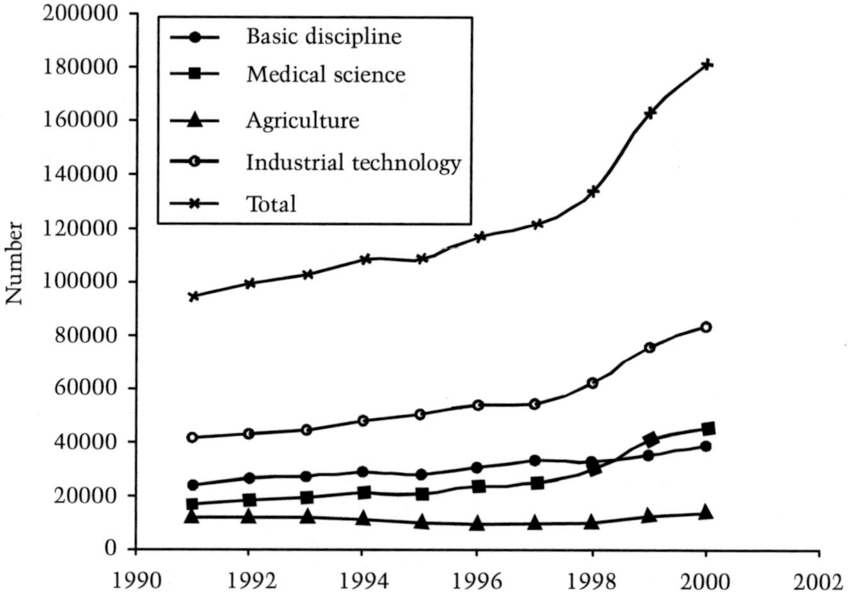

Table 3.8

Numbers of Scientific Papers Published in India and China*

(Number)

Year	*India*	*China*
1980	14983	924
1982	12124	2592
1984	10600	2537
1986	10854	3678
1988	10208	5312
1990	10103	6509
1992	11160	7630
1994	11319	8226
1996	11177	10152
1998	12128	14610
2000	12127	22061

Note: * Data as seen from Science Citation Index.

Source: Based on Arunachalam (2002): 108.

Figure 3.3

Number of Scientific Papers Published by India and China 1980-2000

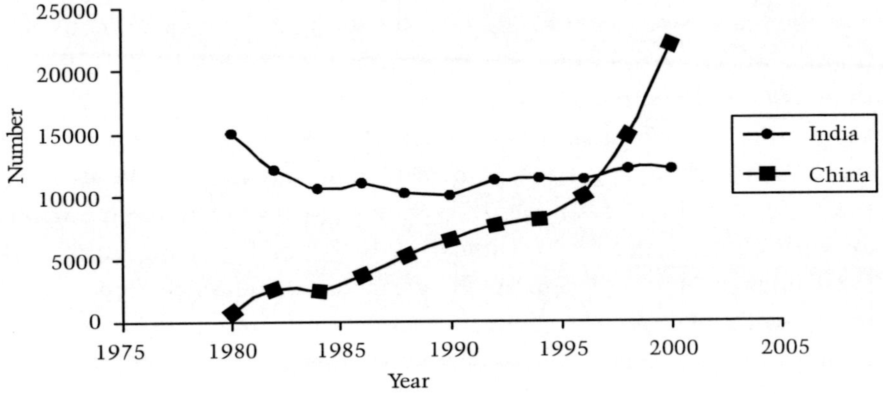

Place, 2003: 2). Table 3.8 and Figure 3.3 indicate a tremendous increase in the number of scientific papers originated in China, as compared to India, in which case it has remained stagnant over the years.

Importance to IPR and Focus on Patents

The linear model of innovation or the 'science push' model (science-technology-economy), based on academic science, which has been governing the science policies and research directions of the scientific communities in developing countries, is losing its relevance in the present scenario of globalisation. There is clear ideological shift from pure academic science to profit oriented science. Scientific communities are reorienting themselves towards creation of wealth from knowledge, resulting in the shift from pure basic research activities to technological innovations completing the whole innovation chain from concept to commercialisation of the knowledge base. This has resulted in enhancement of patenting activity both in India and China. The international regimes like intellectual property rights (IPR) under the WTO and penetration of R&D centres of MNCs into the national economies of the developing countries, particularly India and China, are further catalysing this process patent activity. (Safadi and Laird, 1996).

Over the years, thus, there has been enormous increase in patent activity in China, India is also catching up (Tables 3.9 and 3.10). These tables show a very erratic growth of numbers of patents granted in India over the years from 1980 to 2002 i.e., patents granted decreased in number from 1,746 in 1993-94 to 1,591 patents in the year 2001-02. In China, these increased enormously from 6,556 to 16,297[12] respectively, which is about 10 times more than that for India in the same year. The reasons for the dismal picture of patents granted in India needs to be debated and examined. But at the international level, India seems to have been catching up with China since 1990, indicating better and growing innovative capabilities in India. A recent study by Mahmood and Singh (2003: 1034) point out that US patents granted for inventions made in India increased from 126 during 1990-1994 to 316 during 1995-1999, while in case of China these increased from 239 to 332 during the same period.

Table 3.9

Invention Patents Granted in China, 1985-2006

(Number)

Year	*Total*	*Domestic*	*Percentage*	*Foreign*	*Percentage*
1985-1992	15773	6072	38.5	9701	61.5
1993	6556	2634	40.2	3922	59.8
1994	3883	1659	42.7	2224	57.3
1995	3393	1530	45.0	1863	55.0
1996	2977	1395	46.9	1582	53.1
1997	3494	1532	43.8	1962	56.2
1998	4733	1655	35.0	3078	65.0
1999	7637	3097	40.6	4540	59.4
2000	12683	6177	48.7	6506	51.3
2001	16297	5388	33.0	10909	67.0
2002	21476	5854	27.3	15622	72.7
2003	37154	11404	30.7	25750	69.3
2005	173327	93486	54.0	79842	46.0
2006	210490	122318	58.1	88172	41.9

Sources: MoST, *China Science and Technology Indicators, 2000; 2001; China S&T Statistics Data Book 2007;* State Intellectual Property Office (SIPO), *Statistics for 2001-2003,* Beijing (in Chinese); Wang (2004).

12. These figures are being quoted from Chinese sources, which need to be viewed with certain degree of skepticism. The more authentic figures are inventions patented by India and China in Europe or USA.

Table 3.10

Invention Patents Granted in India, 1980/81-2001/02

(Number)

Year	*Total*	*Domestic*	*Percentage*	*Foreign*	*Percentage*
1980-81	1019	346	34.0	672	66
1981-82	1357	421	31.0	936	69.0
1982-83	1227	405	33.0	822	67.0
1983-84	1320	340	25.8	980	74.2
1984-85	1469	263	17.9	1206	82.1
1985-86	1951	451	23.1	1500	76.9
1986-87	2126	532	25.0	1594	75.0
1987-88	2104	588	27.9	1516	72.1
1988-89	3380	795	23.5	2585	76.5
1989-90	1890	519	27.5	1371	72.5
1990-91	1491	379	25.4	1112	74.6
1991-92	1676	551	32.9	1125	67.1
1992-93	1272	251	19.7	1021	80.3
1993-94	1746	442	25.3	1304	74.7
1994-95	1759	476	27.1	1283	72.9
1995-96	1533	414	27.0	1119	73.0
1996-97	907	293	32.3	614	67.7
1997-98	1844	619	33.6	1225	66.4
1998-99	1800	645	35.8	1155	64.2
1999-2000	1881	557	29.6	1324	70.4
2000-01	1318	399	30.3	919	69.7
2001-02	1591	654	41.1	937	58.9

Sources: Compiled from: *R&D Statistics, 2000-01*. New Delhi 2002, p.100; *www.cagindia.org/reports/scientific/2002*; Patents and Designs in India (2004). *Bulletin of the Intellectual Property Rights*. 9-10(12-1). pp.1-4.

In this regard, one must note the work of the Council of Scientific and Industrial Research (CSIR), a publicly funded autonomous research organisation which has led in commercialisation of inventions. CSIR's foreign patents increased from just 112 in 1998-99 to 728 in 2002-03, while domestic patents increased from 310 to 421 during the same period, proving its enormous innovative capabilities (CSIR, 2004: xii). Compared to the CSIR, the Chinese Academy of Sciences (CAS), has a much larger infrastructure for scientific research; as compared to 38 laboratories and scientific and technical manpower of about 15,000 in the CSIR (2003), (Table 3.12), the CAS had 84 research institutes and scientific and technical manpower of 45,000 (Table 3.11). As for innovative capability judged from the patents filed by these organisations with the USPTO, while Indian CSIR has 728 patents filed by it in the United States Patent and Trademark Office (USPTO), the CAS does not figure in this office in a significant way, except Shanghai Institute of Biochemistry and Cell Biology, Institute of Physics and Beijing Research Institute of Chemistry etc., all under CAS (Mahmood and Singh, 2003). In 2002, CAS was granted 1,001 domestic patents, but only 5 overseas patents (CAS, 2003). However, the number of research papers published by CSIR in 2002-03 was 2012, while that of CAS were five times i.e., 10,165.

Table 3.11

Growth of Chinese Academy of Sciences, 1949-1999

Year	*Research Institutes*	*Total Staff*	*S&T Personnel*
1949	22	575	416
1952	31	5239	3014
1978	72	79755	52045
1985	122	81501	55201
1995	124	75039	58021
1996	123	71763	55523
1997	123	68292	52721*
2002	100	NA	NA
2003	84	NA	45000

Note: **Science* reported 49,000 scientists and engineers in 1997 (*Science* (1997). 277: 761. (8 August).

Source: Data compiled from *Statistical Yearbook of Chinese Academy of Sciences – 2000*. Beijing; *kexue chubanshe*, p.312 (In Chinese); various issues of *China Daily, Beijing Review*; US Embassy in China (2002): 4; Cong (2004): 1.

Thus, in the present scenario of international competition, both these organisations have embarked upon to patent their research results for commercialisation as their main activity and goal, and to consider technology as a market commodity in contrast to the previous paradigm of technology as a social good. This is particularly to China. In both the organisations, recently there has been an attempt to concentrate on resources towards research by reducing their number of research institutions and S&T manpower. While CSIR laboratories have come down from 40 in mid-1990s to 38 in 2003, and the S&T manpower from 19,000 to 15,000; the research institutions under CAS came down from 124 (1995) to 84 (2003) and the S&T manpower came down from 58,000 to 45,000 during the same period.

Table 3.12

Performance of CSIR (1950-51 to 2002-03)

Year	*No. of Laboratories*	*S&T Manpower*	*Paper Published*	*Periodicals*	*Patents*	*Total Expenditure (Rs. million)*
1950-51	11	NA	82	1	18	29.53
1962-63	28	5683	598	27	54	53.39
1972-73	34	10912	1272	57	142	196.14
1982-83	38	10511	2116	NA	93	1015.9
1992-93	40	19207	2591	NA	251	2990.4
2002-03	38	15220	2012	NA	949	10096.5

Source: Annual report of the CSIR for the respective years.

Conclusions

Since 1990s, in China there has been a distinct paradigm shift from egalitarian science, where technology was considered as public good, to entrepreneurial science with a profit motive, where technology is now considered as a private good. This is primarily the result of the open and liberal policies in helping China to face international competition, and due to the fact that a closed system is adverse to innovation. The concept of scientist entrepreneur is well placed in the present environment, although still under experimentation. The exploitation of knowledge for profit has been accepted in China in its system of socialism with 'Chinese characteristics', to the extent that proletariat science is replaced with capitalist science in the Chinese context. The capitalisation of knowledge is part of the productive force that is at the heart of a new mission for the university linking it to the users of knowledge in more effective way. In this new perspective, both China and India are trying to exploit entrepreneurial science to meet socioeconomic goals in their countries. In present day China, socialism with Chinese characteristics means more capitalist science. The moderate political leadership identifies S&T as a major force for economic and social development, and has enthusiastically introduced new programmes with material support for institutionalisation and professionalisation of the scientific research system in China, with a heavily decentralised approach and, commitment with strong supervision by Party committees at various levels. In this process of building up technological innovations, while there are islands of comparable excellence in both India and China, China has been more successful than India in exploiting the international technology market, and linking up academia with enterprises.

References

Arunachalam, S. (2002). "Quality of Science and Science Journals in India", *Current Science* 83(3): 195-196.

Baark, Erik (2001). "The Making of Science and Technology Policy in China", *International Journal of Technology and Management* 21(1/2): 1-21.

———. (1994). "Technological Entrepreneurship and Commercialization of Research Results in the West and in China: Comparative Perspectives", *Technology Analysis & Strategic Management* 6(2): 203-214.

———. (1982). "China's Information Services: A Brief Appraisal of Structures and Policy Issues", *NISSAT Newsletter*, (January-March). pp.4-8.

Balaram, P. (2002). "Bioinformatics: Blowing up a Balloon", *Current Science* 82(10): 1189-1190.

Beijing Review (1994). "Hi-tech Results Seek Industrialisation", *Beijing Review* 37(18): 7.

———. (1993). "Scientific Inventions by College Students", 36(6): 21-23.

———. (1982). "Science Fund Established", *Beijing Review* 25(1): 9.

Chang, P.L. and Hsin-Yu Shih (2004). "The Innovation System of Taiwan and China: A Comparative Analysis", *Technovation* 24(7): 529-539.

China's 5th Place for World S&T Papers (2003). *China Science and Technology Newsletter* 353: 2.

China Daily (1996): 4, October 30.

China Science and Technology Newsletter (1995). *China Science* 63: 3-4. December 15.

Chinese Academy of Sciences (2003). *www.ecdc.net.cn/partners/cas/english.htm* (Downloaded 13 January).

Chopra, K.L. (2004). "Decline of Quality of Science in India", *Current Science* 86(4): 497.

Cong, Cao (2004). *China's Scientific Elite*. London: RoutledgeCurzon. p.256.

Council of Scientific and Industrial Research (CSIR) (2004). *Annual Report 2002-03*. New Delhi: CSIR. p.206.

Cui, Lili (1993). "The Metamorphosis of Beijing University", *Beijing Review* 36(13): 19-22.

CPC Central Committee (1995). *Decision of the Central Committee of the Chinese Communist Party (CCCCP) and the State Council on the Acceleration of Scientific and Technological Progress*. Beijing: State Council. (6 May). p.52.

Feng, Jing (2001). "863 Program Spurs Science and Technology", *Beijing Review* 44(13): 13-17.

Gilboy, G.J. (2004). "The Myth Behind China's Miracle", *Foreign Affairs* 83(4): 33-48.

Gu, Shulin (1995). *Review of Reform Policy for the S&T System in China-From Paid Transactions for Technology to Organizational Restructuring*. Maastricht: UNU/ INTECH. p.61.

———. (1999). *China's Industrial Technology: Market Reform and Organizational Change*. London: Routledge.

———. (2001). "Science and Technology Policy for Development: China's Experience in the Second Half of the Twentieth Century", *Science, Technology & Society* 6(1): 203-234.

Gupta, Y.K. (2002). "Suggestions for Improving the Academic Status of Indian Journals", *Current Science* 83(1): 8-9.

Hua, Kuofeng (1978). "Unite and Strive to Build a Modern Powerful Socialist Country—Report on the Work of the Government. First Session of the 5th National People's Congress, 26 February 1978", *Peking Review* 21(10): 7-40.

Huang, Shiqi (1988). "University Research in China". Paper presented at the International Seminar on *Current Policies for Higher Education Reforms*. Beijing, 21-25 June. p.29.

International Development Research Centre (IDRC) (1997). *A Decade of Reform- Science & Technology Policy in China*. Ottawa: IDRC. p.160.

Jain, N.C. (2000). "Impact Factor of Indian Journals", *Current Science* 79(11): 1513-1514.

Jiang, Zemin (1999). "National Conference Stresses Technological Renovation", *Beijing Review* 42(37): 5.

Kharbanda, V.P and M.A. Qureshi (1987). *Science Technology and Economic Development in China*. New Delhi: Navrang. p.226.

Kharbanda, V.P. (1993). "Analysis of Technological Change at the Firm Level: A Case Study of an Indian Firm", *Journal of Scientific and Industrial Research* 52(9): 585-594.

———. (1996). "Reforming Science and Technology System in China 1985-1995", *Science Technology and Society* 1(1): 145-156.

———. (1999). "Strengthening University-Industry Linkages: Need for Technological Competitiveness in India and China", in V.P. Kharbanda and Ashok Jain (eds.), *Science and Technology Strategies for Development in India and China-A Comparative Study*. New Delhi: Har Anand Publications. pp. 172-208.

———. (2000). "Academia-Industry Symbiosis: Need for Technological Competitiveness in India and China", *China Report* 36(1): 43-709.

———. (2001). "Facilitating Innovation in Indian Small and Medium Enterprises – The Role of Clusters", *Current Science* 80(3): 343-348.

———. (2002). "Learning Organizations: The Process of Innovation and Technological Change", *AI & Society* 16: 89-99.

Kumar, Nagesh (1998). "Tecnology Generation and Technology Transfers I the World Economy: Recent Trends and Implications for Developing Countries", Science, Technology & Society 3(2): 265-306.

Lall, Sanjaya (1998). "Technology and Human Capital in Maturing Asian Countries", *Science, Technology & Society* 3(1): 11-48.

Li, Peng (1996). "Report on the Outline of the Ninth Five Year Plan for National Economic Development and the Long-Range Objectives to the Year 2010", *Beijing Review* 39(15): 1-21.

Macdonald, S. and Yunfeng Deng (2004). "Science Parks in China: A Cautionary Exploration", *International Journal of Technology Intelligence and Planning* 1(1): 1-14.

Mahmood, I.P. and Jasjit Singh (2003). "Technological Dynamism in Asia", *Research Policy* 32(6): 1031-1054.

Mani, Sushil (2002). Government, *Innovation and Technology Policy: An International Comparative Analysis*. Cheltenham, UK: Edward Elgar. p.379.

Mariappan, P. and C. Balasundaram (2002). "Publishing in Indian Journals", *Current Science* 82(2): 115.

Ministry of Science and Technology of the People's Republic of China (MoST) (1998). *Annual Report-1997*. Beijing: MoST. p.14.

———. (2000). *China Science and Technology Indicators 2000*. Beijing: Scientific and Technical Publishing House. pp.1-25.

———. (1993). "Research Institutes Allowed in Foreign Trade", *China Science and Technology Newsletter* 13: 1. (5 December).

———. (1995). "Enterprises Establish Committee University", *China Science and Technology Newsletter* 4. October 15.

Naik, B.M. (1994). "Technology Park and its Relevance to India", *University News* (November 7). p. 65.

OECD (1976). *Science and Technology in People's Republic of China*. Paris: OECD.

Patlibandla, Murali, Deepak Kapur and Bent Peterson (2000). "Import Substitution with Free Trade—Case if India's software industry", *Economic and Political Weekly:* 1263-1270. 8 April.

People's Daily (2003). "China to Build 100 University Science Parks". (17 October).

Raghuram, N. and Y. Madhavi (1997). "Are Indian Scientists Losing in the World Publishing Race?", Paper presented at the *seminar on Emerging Trends in Scientometrics and Informatics*. New Delhi: NISTADS, 6-7 February, p.9.

Ramaseshan, S. (1992). "The Quality of Scientific Journals Published in India—Some Random Thoughts", *Current Science* 63(9&10): 529-534.

Ren, Shengli and Ronald Rousseau (2002). "International Visibility of Chinese Scientific Journals", *Scientometrics* 53(3): 389-405.

Ren, Shengli, Ping Liang and Zu Guangan (1999). "The Challenge for Chinese Scientific Journals", *Science* 286: 1683. 26 November.

Safadi, R. and S. Laird (1996). "The Uruguay Round agreements: Impact on Developing Countries", *World Development* 24(7): 1223-42.

Sandhya, G.D. and Ashok Jain (2003). "Science and Technology Policies for Industrial Development in India", In *Building Technological Capability- Issues and Prospects: Nepal, Bangladesh and India,* Dhaka. The University Press Limited. p.256.

State Science and Technology Commission of The People's Republic of China (SSTC) (1988). *Torch Program—A Program for China's High Technology Industries (huoju jihua)*. Beijing: SSTC. p.5.

Susan, M.W. (2003). *China's Science and Technology Industrial Parks*. Aldershot, Hants: Ashgate. p.220.

Suttmeier, Richard P. (1997). "Recent Developments in the Politics of Chinese Science", *Asian Survey* 17(4): 386.

Tang, Yuankai (2003). "China Becomes Magnet for Foreign—Funded R&D Centers", *Beijing Review* 46(16): 24-25.

Virk, H.S. (2000). "How to Improve Credibility of Indian Journals", *Current Science* 79(10): 1413.

Vohora, S.B., Z.A. Shah and D. Vohora (2001). "Low Impact Factors for Indian Journals—Do Factors other than Quality Influence", *Current Science* 81(8): 867.

Wang, Jun (2004). "Patent Law in China: Two decades later", *Beijing Review* 47(10): 32-33.

Wang, Xiaomin (2000). *Zhongguancun Science Park: A SWOT Analysis*. Institute of Singapore: Southeast Asian Studies. p.42.

Wang, Yuan (2004). "China's Government R&D Institutes in Changes and Associated Issues", *Science Technology and Society:* 171-207. (July-December).

Wei, Liming (1993). "Torch Program—Making Rapid Progress", *Beijing Review* 36(10): 18-23.

White, S., Jian Gao and Wei Zhang (2002). "China's Venture Capital Industry: Institutional Trajectories and System Structure". Paper Presented at the International Conference on *Financial Systems, Corporate Investment in Innovation and Venture Capital*, Brussels, p.25. 7-8 November.

Yang, Anxian, Shen Aiqun, V.V. Krishna and V.P. Kharbanda (1997). "Twists and Turns in the Formation of Chinese Scientific Community", in Jacques Gaillard, V.V. Krishna and Roland Waast (eds.), *Scientific Communities in the Developing World*. New Delhi; Sage. p.207-235.

Zedtwitz, Maximilian von (2004). "Managing Foreign R&D Laboratories in China", *R&D Management* 34(4): 439-466.

Zhao, Ziyang (1985). "Speech to the National Science and Technology Conference", *Xinhua* in Chinese, 20 March, *Summary of World Broadcasts*/FE/7908/BII/1-7.

Zhu, Rongji (1999). "Report on the Work of the Government", *Beijing Review* 42(14): 10-25.

Acknowledgements: The main contents of this paper have been heavily drawn from my thesis work submitted at the Jawaharlal Nehru University, New Delhi in 2004. I sincerely thank Director, NAM S&T Centre, India Habitat Centre, New Delhi for providing me the infrastructural facilities to write this paper. I am also thankful to Mr. Garauv Gaur, Research Assistant, NAM S&T Centre, for helping me in the preparation of power point slides.

4 China: The Energy Picture

Sudha Mahalingam

We need first to consider that China is the second largest energy consumer in the world, particularly of oil, and in due course, it might become the largest. In 2006, 70 per cent of China's oil consumption was accounted for industry, 10 per cent by the commercial sector, and 7 per cent by transportation. This pattern is not at all counter-intuitive because China has pursued an export oriented and manufacturing-based growth; industry, and naturally, has been a huge consumer of energy. Nor is it surprising that the commercial sector gobbles up large amounts of energy, with all the huge malls and shopping complexes which China is building along with the other products of urbanisation. While transportation accounts for only 7 per cent of total energy consumption, about half of all oil utilisation is in this sector. With per capita oil consumption being very low, it is inevitable that China's overall oil consumption should be increasing in geometric progression. Having said this, it is also important to note that the distribution of consumption is skewed as it is in India. It is the urban rich who have seized the biggest share of energy, which is far higher than that of the rural population. Thus, for many years, energy intensity estimates were pegged at only half of GDP, according to Chinese official figures and data from the International Energy Agency (IEA). Those estimates fell by the wayside beginning in 2001. Energy consumption started growing much faster, running almost completely parallel with GDP growth, largely because of inefficient energy use and energy intensive industries.

It is very obvious that urbanisation has played a huge part in putting China in its current global spot. In 1990, only 26 per cent of China was urbanised; today the figure is 43 per cent. Consumption rates go up with urbanisation, given that in urban areas, energy use is 3.5 times that in rural areas. Metropolitan areas usually involve the building of high-rise residential apartments, whose basic requirements include steel, cement, glass and chrome, all of them using high amounts of energy. Moreover, there is water to be pumped into urban high-rise residential areas, and electricity as well as large amounts of cooking fuel are to be provided.

The second factor behind the rise in energy consumption of China is the roads that are being built all over China along with the very large number of automobiles in the big cities especially in Beijing and Shanghai. Anywhere from eight to nine million cars are registered annually; according to one estimate, 370 million cars will be plying on China's roads by 2030 which is a staggering number. Oil consumption will increase even more, with transport consuming some 66 per cent of all oil in the next 10 years or so. Coal demand—mainly to provide electricity—is also going up by 12 per cent annually. Oil demand is growing by 9 per cent annually, and natural gas, by 15 per cent. The consumption of the various sources of energy is constrained only by supply.

The other main reason why China's energy consumption is growing is pricing. Like India, China has not priced its energy rationally, pegging costs at much lower rates than most other countries. China's prices are lower than those in South Korea, for example, as well as in Japan, Mongolia, India, and various countries in Europe, and higher only than in the US. A country which is importing, say, half of its oil requirements and does not link the price of that imported commodity to global prices, may be heading for trouble. In India, the basic energy price demand of a citizen is much lower than it should be. However, because of the huge tax on petroleum products, the price works out to almost the same as the highest level in Europe. China does not impose the same level of taxes on energy as does India. The other obvious factor is that there is excessive dependence on coal in China. A corollary is the problem caused by the lack of railway infrastructure to help shift coal from the mining regions in north and northwest to the south and southeast consuming centres, and the reluctance to improve the railway network and address pollution issues.

China's oil reserves are depleting; the last major find was Daching. China is now importing most of its oil and gas requirements. Oil imports are currently around 50 per cent of China's consumption, or about five million barrels per day (bpd). The US is importing around 10 million bpd and consuming 20 million bpd. China is thus still far behind the US in dependence on imports; yet it is the second largest consumer of oil. Its fuel imports alone will jump to 13 million bpd by 2030, according to IEA, assuming that current trends continue. The Persian Gulf nations supply the bulk of China's oil imports, much as they do for India. For India, this is about two-third of all requirements, the corresponding figure for China is 45 per cent. Africa, surprisingly, takes care of about 33 per cent of China's oil consumption and Russia, 8 per cent. By 2020, according to IEA estimates China's oil imports will go up to two-third (68 per cent). The gas supply gap is about 10 billion cubic metres at present, and is expected to rise to 50 billion cubic metres. Besides import-dependence, this also implies soaring energy bills. Even if crude oil prices are assumed to be at US $60 a barrel, China's import bill could be anything like US $100 billion annually. Added to that is price volatility. Economic planning simply becomes more difficult with price fluctuations. Prices are now hardening: sometime ago, they were around 40, and now they have gone above 60, and this fluctuation is worrisome. The sea routes are problematic too—around 80 per cent of China's imports will have to pass through the Malacca Straits and that is a major worry. Recently the Indian Navy made it known that it would like to sit astride the Indian Ocean, so that we could acquire the capacity to block supplies, and other countries are also likely to be looking at such an option. China does not have a blue water Navy that can ensure security of transport.

What is China doing to deal with all of this? One of China's major problems is the lack of coordination in energy policymaking. There are simply too many players, and the state-owned enterprises and national oil companies are very much satraps in their own right and do not listen to the government. Even if the Chinese situation will allow the leadership to impose discipline on these players, there is yet another problem: i.e., the State is unable to make up its mind on whether energy is a strategic commodity, and therefore must be subject to a command and control regime, or is it best left to the market. The basic dilemma is that China's policies are very fluid; they do not effectively enable the market to take charge of initiating price reforms and related activities. There is also a perception of vulnerability which is very important. The Middle East region is uniformly described as 'unstable'. Yet if the Middle East were indeed unstable, then why is it that for 200 years now, there has not been a single occasion when oil supplies were disrupted, even through a number of wars and conflicts? It appears that the real time opportunity for disruption is through piracy or is a terrorist attack; as prefigured in the attack on the Rusta Nura Terminal in Saudi Arabia, an event which could have deprived the market of some eight or nine million barrels of oil daily. Otherwise, there has never been any conscious disruption of supplies. This bogey was raised following the 9/11 attacks in America, and since then the issue of supply disruption has become a constant source of worry for policymakers. The Chinese leadership, too, is influenced by this fear of potential supply disruption. This is a very important factor determining their energy security thinking and strategy.

A basic question is what is special about China in regard to Energy policy—China is doing very much what everybody else is doing! Firstly, it is trying to diversify its sources of energy supply, a fundamental solution available to any country that may be starved of energy. The US has done the same, sourcing its supply from Canada, Mexico, Venezuela and Western Africa. Europe is now sourcing most of its oil from Russia. For its part, China is tapping supplies from Africa, Latin America and Canada. It is doing so through the acquisition of overseas oil equity; this is however only one route. More importantly, China is entering into bilateral long-term contracts for the purchase of oil from these countries. That contributes more to energy security than the purchase of oil assets, which for various reasons should be more of a commercial than a strategic decision.

The second strategy for China is, that once it has diversified its sources of supply, it could reduce the congestion in the Malacca Straits. It could then use new sea routes i.e., the Pacific. While supplies from Africa will still have to go through Malacca, the supply from Latin America, and perhaps Canada, could take the Pacific route; further if the Arctic ice cap melts, and the northern channels open up, and there could be a third route.

The third component of China's emerging energy strategy is the laying of pipelines to leverage its land power. This is a typical response which Europe has also used quite successfully: Europe has built pipelines connecting it with Russia, and now they are connecting to Central Asia from Azerbaijan, as well as from Russia to Europe. There are pipelines from

North Africa to Europe to Italy and to Spain (and for that matter, pipelines between Bolivia and Argentina). Any land power which has access to neighbours who have energy will want the pipeline route; once there is a pipeline, an adversary cannot divert supplies and you build security. India, unfortunately, has not been able to build pipelines in our neighbourhood despite being ringed by gas-rich countries. China's pipelines include the East Siberian-Pacific Ocean Oil Pipeline (ESPO) which is very important as it can access Russia's Far East and the Siberia, which form part of the emerging oil frontier. For three to four years, Russia was stringing along both China and Japan as competitors for this pipeline, breathing hot and cold. Russia conveyed in the first place that it would want the pipeline to be built up to Nakhodka; subsequently they had indicated a preference for Daching as the terminus (the first variant would favour Japan and the second would help China). In the outcome, Russia settled for Nakhodka, from where the oil could be shipped even to the USA. China, however, has continued to stress Daching. It is believed that this option was clinched through the offer of a loan to Rosneft (a major state oil company in Russia) of US $35 billion at 6 per cent interest. One should not forget that it was Chinese funding a few years ago which had 'given Rosneft effective clout (China had helped Rosneft acquire Yukos assets when Yukos was dismembered). This helpful act had prepared the ground for Russia agreeing to China's demand to build the spur from the main pipeline, connecting it to Daching. This could help China secure 20 million tonnes of Russian oil in export annually for the next 20 years. One also has to keep in mind the Altai gas pipeline which the then President Vladimir Putin had proposed a few years ago—projected to be 6,700 km long (perhaps the longest oil pipeline of all time). This proposal has now been revived, and a joint venture between China National Petroleum Corporation (CNPC) and Russia's Gazprom has reportedly been set up to take this venture forward. In return, China has agreed to give Gazprom marketing rights within China. Historically, China has not encouraged foreign investment in its exploration and production sector, nor has it encouraged investment in its refinery and exploration sector. An exception has now been made in favour of Gazprom. A related aspect is the development of China's cooperation with Kazakhstan in the oil/natural gas sector. It is a notable here too, China is actively pursuing a policy of export credits, credit guarantees, in return for commitment to build oil and gas pipelines. Thus, the Atasu-Alashankou pipeline, it is reported, will be extended further to the Caspean Sea. This pipeline, already functional, reaches the Central part of Kazakhstan. We should also take note of the pipeline building activity in the Myanmar-Yünnan region. It is understood that CNPC will be building this 2,400 km long gas pipeline from Situ in the south of Myanmar, all the way to the north connecting with Yunnan. Part of the trade-off would be continuous political and diplomatic support to Myanmar which is a factor of tremendous importance to the Myanmar regime's very survival. Also noteworthy is the reported abandonment of the Kra Canal Project (across the Isthmus of Kra). It was envisaged that this would save about 700 nautical miles for oil/ gas tankers plying through this region.

We also need to assess the utility to China of its overseas oil/gas investments, i.e., through acquisitions of leases by CNPC, China National Offshore Oil Corporation (CNOOC), China Petroleum and Chemical Corporation (Sinopec), China International Trust and Investment Corporation (CITIC) and Zhenhua Oil Corporation reportedly totalling about US $20 billion by the end of 2008. About 600,000 bpd are being produced in these oilfields by Chinese companies, but little, is actually going back to China. This is not abnormal: because the global oil market is fungible—i.e., you can buy oil anywhere and a preferential price is available only if one is an operator—with a specific provision written into the contract for sale at a preferential price over a particular period. Apart from the obvious discouragement of the distant location of these acquisitions overseas, one also has to consider whether oil produced at these locations is suitable for China's refineries. Overall, these and other factors make overseas oil equity investments a doubtful proposition as an energy security measure. One reason why China is going overseas to acquire oil leases, is that its national oil companies have two million employees and they do not have to pay dividends to the government. They need to invest their huge monopoly profits as well as export their manpower and expertise. In this context, overseas oil acreages are considered quest profitable. However, creeping expropriation or outright nationalisation is a potential threat which China might have to deal with.

Also of interest in this context is China's Africa connection. China is very much part of Africa's growth story, China's FDI in Africa is said to be US $60 billion per year. At the same time China also has a collateral strategic interest of its own—because Africa provides access to strategic minerals and other raw materials which would feed China's own growth. China has provided integrated packages of aid, loans, infrastructure construction (hospitals, railways, telecommunication, training and other sectors, etc.) to several countries in Africa. Preferential tariffs have been provided for, to help import Africa's commodity products. Chinese companies also receive some governmental support.

What are the prospects of China diversifying its sources of supply? By 2020, the Middle East would be able to supply as much as 50 per cent, Africa 25 per cent and Russia, a much higher percentage than it is supplying at present. (Possibly up from 8 per cent to 20-25 per cent.) China can also turn to its own backyard to augment its energy supply.

Why is China's energy quest bothering the US? There are some misconceptions about the China 'threat'. In its quest, China cannot lock up and divert energy supplies, because oil markets do not function in a way that this can be done. Oil markets are truly global and evolved and any increase in production following a discovery by Chinese companies anywhere in Africa or elsewhere will actually add to the global pool of oil and energy, and many countries could benefit from this.

What are China's other responses to the Energy security problem. Regarding price reform, China does not actually want to reduce prices. It appears to have worked out a via media i.e., if the crude price exceeds US $80, then the refineries will absorb the increase, and retail prices will not be increased. It also has at its disposal Energy Law (2007). This is however, inadequate as it does not set targets and a time frame. The government is seeking to fix the responsibility on its officials for ensuring energy supply to the purchaser. It is also looking at the futures market; this would be a constructive idea, considering that China procures a considerable amount of oil from the spot markets. It would then be able to hedge its risks. However, this may not be worthwhile as the RMB (currency: renminbi) is not convertible. There is also an effort at strengthening institutions e.g., the abolition of the Ministry of Energy, persuading and encouraging the national oil companies to diversify and compete with each other. Besides, China is also building a strategic petroleum reserve.

In conclusion, China's energy import dependence is difficult to contain or reverse and China has to learn to live with it. Regarding overseas oil assets, it is difficult to escape the conclusion that the current acquisitions referred to above will not help China ensure energy security. What is more likely to help is the building of pipelines and hydel projects such as the Three Gorges. Most of all, internal pricing and policy reforms are critical requirements for energy security. In the absence of these elements, China lacks a coherent or coordinated energy strategy.

5 China's Challenges in Environment and Development

Prodipto Ghosh

The following paragraphs on the theme 'China's environment' incorporate a 'strategic' perspective as required. This is not derived however from mainstream writings on China, but rather, from the energy and climate change literature, with which I am familiar. There is apparently, some kind of intellectual consensus within China that the attributes of national power include military strength which, in turn, depends on population and human capital, control of natural resources, including energy. This may explain some of China's actions regarding overseas acquisitions and carbon space, without which any control of energy resources becomes meaningless. They are also very clear about the need to focus on natural resources and a clean environment as these are the basis for the existence and development of a society. Having said that, however, Chinese policymakers are well aware that their model of economic growth has resulted in severe environmental problems that create obstacles to the country's development.

In the context of China's interaction with the environment, the relevant point is not merely China's large territorial expanse, but the fact that nearly two-third of China is mountainous, compared to one-fifth in the case of India. Also, arable land in China is only 11 per cent of its total land area; in our case, it is 53.7 per cent, and the practice of double-cropping in many areas with arable land resources reinforces the advantage we have over China in this respect. As against this, China has vast areas of pasture land, which we do not. Their forest resources, however, are similar to ours. Like India, China is vulnerable to a host of natural disasters, including those relating to water. The leading concerns in this respect are surface water run-off and soil erosion. Although China is three times the size of India, in terms of aggregate fresh water resources they are only marginally better placed. India is also much better endowed in terms of surface water and ground water. Overall, China is a water-stressed country with only less than 25 per cent of the global average for water.

Natural Resources

I have used two different figures for hydro-power capacity: one is from the United Nations, which seems more credible. The Chinese have a much higher figure, which I quote in another part of my paper. Even with UN's lower figure, however, it is obvious that China has the highest hydro-power capacity in the world. In terms of species diversity, China, very much like India, is a mega-diverse region. India has two mega-diverse hotspots, while China has only one. China has a very wide portfolio of minerals: more than 171 minerals have been found in commercial quantities across the country, out of which 159 have been subjected to a census. A point of special interest relates to lithium deposits: it turns out that China and Bolivia essentially have a global monopoly on lithium, an extremely important element in the energy contest, as it is the key component in high-density storage batteries which may power the next generation of automobiles. Overall, China's mineral base is significant but not abundant, i.e., a situation very similar to India's. Both countries are rich in coal and relatively poor in petroleum resources. For exact figures for China's hydro-power resources one has to depend on official Chinese sources, which are not reliable. Suffice it to say that China is well-endowed with hydel resources as well. They also have a huge potential for solar, wind and biomass. They are much better placed than India in terms of wind resources, though not as well placed in the solar and biomass sector.

Demographic Patterns

In terms of demographic trends, the important point is that both countries have a demographic dividend. While their dependency ratios are coming down, the indication is that India's will be sustained for much longer. Somewhere close to 2030, India will overtake China in population, but we will maintain a demographic dividend for at least 25 or 30 years longer than China, giving us an opportunity to catch up on growth.

It is well known that China has done much better than India in both economic development and human development. In the last years of the Tenth Five-Year Plan (2002-2007), however, India did not do too badly either. The specific feature of Chinese growth is the dominance of heavy industries in the secondary sector. For India, it is the services sector that is rapidly rising, particularly information technology and IT-enabled services, of which we have 65 per cent and 46 per cent of the global market, respectively. All of these patterns have a bearing on the variety of environmental challenges that we face.

Environmental Challenges

Some of the key environmental challenges are essentially common to both India and China. China has a much higher energy intensity of the economy than India. Our current energy intensity is approximately at the same level as in the EU. Indeed, we are doing better than many of the EU countries with our energy intensity by a declining trend, whereas China's position is more haphazard. Coal and oil are likely to dominate China's energy requirements in the future, as it is for India. However, the rapid economic growth has come at significant environmental cost; official figures from China estimate that the ecological damage amounts to between 3.5 to 7 per cent of the GDP. Thus if you go behind the façade of heavy infrastructure, consumption goods and other indicators of China's growth, the devastation of natural resources pulls down their real GDP growth rate to a point where it might well approximate that of India.

Ecological Footprint

India's ecological footprint is estimated at 6 per cent, while China's is 16 per cent, which is similar to that of the US. Any discussion of environmental footprints depends to a certain extent on mythology and on specific assumptions. Thus, quite a different story is told by National Geographic's Greendex: based on this index—which makes an assessment of a country's level of environmental sustainability and consumption—India is ranked 1st, Brazil is 2nd, China is 3rd, and the US is last in the list. (Most industrialised countries are clustered at the bottom of the ranking.)

Water Resources

Many of China's concerns in the area of water are very similar to ours. The utilisation of water resources has gradually been increasing in China, and today we are speaking of a billion cubic metres. Both industrial and domestic use patterns have been on the rise, with domestic use being higher. In the case of India, the characteristic feature of the country's water resources is the sharp increase in ground water resources, as well as the contamination by arsenic and fluoride over many states. This is clearly a serious problem as far as drinking water is concerned.

China and India's common concerns include the enforcement of existing laws, to ensure adherence to water quality standards, and insufficient coordination among the line ministries and departments handling the resource. In India, there are at least six ministries handling various aspects of water resources and incentive-based instruments are generally not being applied. However, China is gradually moving from concentration control of total pollutants, to discharges and emissions permits, as incentive-based instruments are gradually being introduced.

Air Quality

It is in this area that China and India show a marked difference. To begin with, the two countries have varying criteria in terms of pollution levels. For example, China's Grade 1 is Grade 2 in India's case. What we do find is that overall, in terms of urban air pollution, our critical concern is PM10 (respirable particulate matter), that is, very fine particulate matter which one breathes in and which causes lung damage. In China, it is the emission of sulphur dioxide and nitric oxide which result in urban pollution (smog), leading to very high levels of respiratory diseases and also acid rain. China has faced wide criticisms from its neighbours for the acid rain problem. Of course, this problem has been handled cooperatively; this is not the forum, however, for discussing how it was handled. The major sources of this type of pollution are industry and transport, as is the case in India, except that biomass burning is done to a higher degree here. These are some of the common concerns—emissions from the growing vehicular fleet, dependence on coal for power generation, industrial air pollution etc.

Solid Waste

Our problems are, again, quite comparable, in the area of solid waste generation, although China's are much larger in scale. Common concerns include the following: inadequate industrial waste segregation and recycling; disposal in open land, causing land pollution and water pollution; e-waste management; and the inadequacy of regulation to promote segregation, use, recycling and safe disposal of industrial waste. Both India and China segregate their domestic waste, and the remediation and rehabilitation of polluted sites—including waste disposal dumps—is also a serious issue in both countries.

Forestry

India's forests have a lower productivity than China's; this is because a much larger part comprises stable natural forests. Overall, India has a somewhat higher forest cover than China, but China has a more aggressive programme for afforestation. Significantly, China has thought it fit to involve the private sector in its afforestation process, whereas in India, the involvement of the private sector in such programmes seems to have faced serious political roadblocks. India's forest cover is estimated at 20.6 per cent and is considered stable, and in fact is increasing very slightly. China's forest cover, meanwhile, is at 18.21 per cent and is also increasing with the help of the aggressive afforestation programme it has started. There are common concerns such as the following: high pressure on forests; both countries are net importers of timber; degradation of natural forests; and both countries are concerned about the possible impact of climate change on species distribution and productivity. The principal interest with respect to forest resources in both countries is the maintenance of water resources.

Biodiversity and Traditional Knowledge

India is better endowed than China in biodiversity. While both countries have rich traditions of indigeneous medicine based on biodiversity, India seems to have gone further in taking of national-level initiatives for recognising traditional knowledge, as well as putting in place legislative provisions and institutional mechanisms for the protection of biodiversity and traditional knowledge.

Climate Change: Impact on Biodiversity and Livelihood

Environmental Governance

Although the structures of government are different in China, it has, like India, elaborate regulatory systems for the environment. In both countries, there is a big problem with enforcement and monitoring. China, however, seems to be ahead of India in terms of preparation of regional environmental plans, regional environmental impact assessments as well as regional enforcement and monitoring. Note that both countries are signatories to major multilateral economic agreements.

Climate Change

I begin this discussion on climate change by making clear my conviction that it is real, and in fact, is a very serious environmental issue that poses dire challenges to humanity. If it is not addressed effectively, and in time, beginning in the next two decades, climate change has the potential to alter the very nature of human civilisation. This is in no way an exaggeration. The other thing that we need to keep in mind, is that climate change could be said to be the mother of all other economic issues of our time. In terms of implications for the future international division of economic labour, global warming dwarfs other processes such as the World Trade Organization (WTO). Why is climate change more significant than the WTO? Because when we are talking of addressing climate change, in the first instance, we are talking of rationing the global use of energy; and we assume that to begin with, the right to use energy, relates directly to a nation's economic capacity and economic growth potential. The sheer scale of the economic impact becomes even more magnified, when one considers sectors such as water resources and agriculture.

The overarching issues on climate change are similar in nature for India and China; the differences lie in the scale of the changes that have been discussed, and the response strategies which are drawn from these countries' restrictive trajectories of development. There are differences between us; but they are essentially about scale and do not amount to a change in perspective as to how the problems are to be addressed. Some comparisons, mostly well-known, are relevant at this point:

- India has a much larger population without access to electricity.
- In terms of per capita emissions, India is about a little more than one-third that of China.
- In both countries, the energy sector accounts for the highest volume of greenhouse gas (GHG) emissions.
- India's growth in primary energy supply over the last decade has been a low of 5 per cent per annum, whereas in China, it is 7 per cent.
- China's energy intensity is decreasing at a much lower rate than that of India.
- Both countries are coal dependent, with India at a lower scale than China: 53 per cent of India's total power generation capacity is based on coal, against 78 per cent for China.
- Industry is the largest end-user in both countries, but with respect to intensity, in India there has been a continuous decline since 1980, and comparable to the EU 15 at present. In China it has been quite haphazard.

Dr. Sudha Mahalingam has discussed energy prices. There is another way of looking at energy prices. This is indicated in the figures from the International Energy Agency (IEA) showing the retail prices of electricity. For example, if one takes the figure for gasoline, as a percentage or number of times that of per capita GDP, India has by far the world's most expensive energy. As a percentage of India's income, the energy prices in the country are the highest in the world, more than double that of Turkey which is second in rank. By this measure, China also has a much higher energy price than all the developed countries. This means that consumers are lot more careful with the use of energy, a lot more conscious about the need to conserve energy than in the case of developed countries. It also shows that industry has a much higher incentive to shift away from energy-intensive technologies to labour-intensive technologies than would otherwise be the case. Of course, in this calculation, one needs to take into account relative capital prices. Overall labour prices are cheap and capital and energy prices are high.

Projections

Under various scenarios, China would probably double its primary energy requirements between 2006 and 2030. This would work out to 5.1 billion tonnes of coal equivalent (tce). This is based on a recent exercise done jointly by National Council of Applied Economic Research (NCAER) and The Energy Resources Institute (TERI) using two different models. It shows that in India it would be somewhat less than 1.4 billion tce, so that in 2030, the country would still be at about one-third that of China in terms of commercial energy intensity.

I now come to the clean development mechanism (CDM) and participation in the carbon market. Today China has a larger number of registered CDM projects than India. In global ranking, India is in second place. During the first four years of the CDM regime, India was ahead of China in the number of CDM projects, even though the energy sector—as Prem Shankar Jha mentioned earlier—was responsible for about one-sixth of these projects. (The CDM is an arrangement under the Kyoto Protocol by which countrics that do not havc GHG mitigation commitments, either undertake a project which they would not otherwise take on, or put in place a technology which they would not otherwise adopt, thus resulting in a reduction of their levels of emission. For example, if a country shifts from coal to gas—and thereby emits, for the same million kilowatt hours of electricity, about half the amount of electricity—then that saving is certified through an international regulatory process and this can be sold in a global market to countries which have made binding commitments to reduce their emissions.) In this market, India is number 2, and by a long shot. In terms of the actual credits for registered projects, however, India is well behind China and there are two reasons for this. First, typically, Chinese plants are much larger and involve much higher use of coal and fossil energy than Indian plants and therefore individual CDM projects are much bigger. Second, there is the specific issue of HFC-23, a particular byproduct of the manufacture of refrigerant gases, which on disposal through the CDM route results in a very high generation of carbon revenue (CRs). China had a much higher pre-existing capacity for HFC-23 than India.

Climate Change Concerns

These are very similar for both India and China. First of all, energy consumption as well as associated GHG gases are expected to increase. Coal will continue to be the main source of energy and is the most carbon intensive fossil fuel. Energy security in both countries is a major challenge. How to address climate change without recourse to coal which is what both countries essentially have in significant quantity. Improvement in energy efficiency is of key importance for both countries, and among the leading options is the increasing share of renewables in the primary energy supply. In the case of China, it needs to look at structural changes in the economy. Energy efficient renewable energy sources must be promoted: biomass, wind, solar and nuclear. India needs to look at transport infrastructure to encourage a model shift away from a very rapidly growing personal transportation preferences and promotion of renewables besides three-stage nuclear. Three-stage nuclear is a technology that China does not have and probably does not need, but India needs it, and fortunately has developed it, along with enhancements in energy efficiency and energy-intensive industries. It should also be noted that India's irrigation sector is markedly less efficient in terms of energy use compared to China's.

Impact

Climate change will have a huge impact on both countries, given the climate-related dependence of sectors which are crucial for livelihood—primarily agriculture, animal husbandry and fishing. In both countries, there is a large population dependent on agriculture, and this sector makes a significant contribution towards GDP, which is even greater in the case of India than in China. Irrigation is a major consumer of water in both cases and, of course, both countries are susceptible to coastal environmental risks.

Political Perspectives

The following are some of the key issues for both developed and developing countries, in the climate change negotiations. The terminology used for the developed world is 'Annex I', and for the developing countries, 'non-Annex I'. The perspectives that we had suggested at the negotiations, and which will be recapitulated here are common to both China and India. In the current negotiations, there is a question of the long-term shared vision for addressing climate change. The developed countries see this essentially as setting a numerical target and time frame for GHG stabilisation. They speak frequently of 450 parts per million (ppm) by 2050, for the non-Annex I countries (this includes India and China). Both believe that it must necessarily include all the building blocks which are involved in the current negotiations, i.e., mitigation, adaptation technology, finance, as well as the basis for allocations of GHG entitlements across parties and the time frame in which these entitlements would be realised. What is crucial is not merely how big the common pie is going to be locally, but how it is going to be shared, i.e., who gets what at each point in time? There are major differences in perspective in this regard.

In terms of GHG mitigation actions, the Annex I countries propose that both developed and 'key developing countries'—a collective term for China, India, Brazil and South Africa—need to take on legally binding commitments for GHG mitigation. However, the nature and extent of commitments by developed and developing countries may differ. Their essential position is that the developed countries and the 'key developing countries' differ only in the scale of actions required, not in their nature. The developing countries believe that developed countries need to commit to deep, long-term, legally binding GHG reductions consistent with the espoused scale and time frame of GHG stabilisation. Thus if they are saying that they have to stabilise at 450 ppm by 2050, then such action had better be seen starting in 2020. GHG mitigation actions by developing countries must be enabled and compensated by financial transfers and technology from developed countries, and there is no question of a so-called 'mezzanine floor' for key developing countries.

On the nature of the developing country actions: according to the developed countries, developing country mitigation actions can take the form of legal commitments on sectoral targets, or technology mandates (which Japan favours) or low carbon development. This is a euphemism for essentially a carbon cap by the EU. There are basic energy intensity improvements which the US has often articulated. The Annex I countries maintain that in any event 'key developing countries' have to accept these commitments. The non-Annex I countries have pointed out that sectoral targets or technology mandates would lead to market capture by Annex I companies and increase costs appreciably. They are also impractical, given the great heterogeneity among the developing countries. Hence one has to provide for differentiation among them. Thus the energy and carbon intensity of many developing countries are already comparable to, or in some cases better than that of developed countries. In any case the developing countries have little historical responsibility. (The question of historical responsibility has come out as a very salient issue during the last round of negotiations.)

Nationally Appropriate Mitigation Actions (NAMAs) to be taken by developing countries is one of the provisions in the Bali Action Plan (2007). According to the developed countries, the NAMAs of developing countries must be scrutinised by an international panel and the level of ambition may be adjusted by that international panel. NAMAs may be funded nationally. There may be need for support from a financial mechanism i.e., financial mechanism which is being set up is intended to be set up under the climate change regime and also funded from the carbon market in which case it is offloaded to the private sector and all NAMA actions are subject to monitoring, reporting and verification and not only those that receive support. The non-Annex I nations believe that the mitigation actions are to be formulated by developing countries concerned without external review and only those NAMA actions that are enabled by finance, technology and capacity building are subject to accountability in the sense of monitoring, reporting and verification, together with the support received. So, no money, no review of actions. And if actions are undertaken with inflow of money and technology, then the money and technology are also monitored and reviewed.

In terms of financial transfers, the Annex I propose that financial transfers would serve as aid to some developing countries at the discretion of developed countries and largely administered by the World Bank, regional development banks, and bilateral agencies. They may be raised as the share of the carbon allocations for the developed countries or through a carbon tax. This is the Swiss proposal. On the other hand, the Annex I countries maintain that financial transfers are not to be treated as aid in respect of climate change. There must be a new and additional and over and above the 0.7 per cent of official development assistance (ODA). These must be based on assessed contributions and not discretionary, and must be administered by a financial mechanism answerable to the parties. The nomenclature for that body is Conference of the Parties serving as the Meeting of the Parties (COP/MOP), with a unique governing structure that is to be negotiated and the extent of financial contributions that are needed are 0.5 to 1 per cent of the aggregate GDP of all developed countries. Essentially, we are insisting that there should be no uncompensated mitigation actions. It would be very difficult to carry out our actions without compensation. Further there are things which we are doing on our own and we do not pose these for financial transfers or technology transfers, such actions are not subject to international review. Over the years, the positions on both sides have become very rigid. We are now in a situation when each side can accurately read the language on the other side, and on this basis we have not detected any significant shift on the other side. Neither have they detected any significant shift on our side over the last several years.

Moreover, the Annex I nations believe that technology transfers must fully respect the intellectual property rights (IPR) of the holders, and that the only issue with respect to technology transfer is reduction or elimination of tariffs on equipment embodying clean technology imposed by the developing countries. These countries have yet worked out a position on the purchase of IPRs through the financial mechanism. What the non-Annex I countries are saying is that technology transfers must include the following: invocation of compulsory licensing with negotiated licence fees, purchase of the relevant IPRs licences by the financial mechanism, collaborative R&D between institutions in developed and developing countries with IPR sharing and financing by the financial mechanism, and a network of regional technology innovation centres in developing countries to promote collaborative R&D capacity building and employment. The Annex I countries have no firm position yet on collaborative R&D, but they are positive on regional technology innovation centres.

The Annex I countries have been speaking about mainstreaming adaptation actions in development plans. What this means is that there has to be an internal diversion of resources away from development as is generally understood, to significantly address adaptation actions. However, least developed countries (LDCs) and SIDS (small island developing states) may be provided some funding for adaptation.

Non-Annex I countries have taken the position that there should be no diversion of development resources to address climate change. All vulnerable regions will receive adaptation funding from the financial mechanism i.e., this will not be limited to some special countries. The required resources would be of the same order as for mitigation and this judgement is based on actually our own experience in deployment of our fiscal resources.

Equally important is the issue of lifestyle changes. Non-Annex I's position is that the high level of per capita GHG emissions in developed countries is the inevitable outcome of unsustainable lifestyles, comprising unsustainable patterns of production and consumption and the peculiar needs to be addressed in future arrangements.

6 China's External Economic Relations and Position on Leading International Economic Issues

D.S. Rajan

Firm linkages have always existed between the domestic goals and foreign policy directions of the People's Republic of China (PRC). In the current period, the objective of building a 'harmonious socialist society' at home is being matched by a foreign policy course aimed at creating a 'harmonious world', providing China a 'win-win' relationship with the external world. As a corollary, the linkage between China's internal development objectives and its external economic relations has continued intact. Overall, the reforms and opening up in the country in vogue since 1978, has produced results: emergence of a middle class capable of contributing to the GDP growth through consumption and more importantly, the establishment of an export-led economy. China registered an average annual growth of 9.6 per cent in the post reform period, an unprecedented achievement among the developing nations. With 13 per cent growth in 2007, as revised by China in January 2009, the country has overtaken Germany as the world's third largest economy. China's share in the global GDP has increased. (From 1 per cent in 1978 to over 5 per cent in 2007); its share in global trade also jumped (from less than 1 per cent in 1978 to 8 per cent in 2008).[1]

Three stages are discernible in China's internal and external economic strategy in the post reform period.

- In the first stage (1978-2005), the Chinese economy grew at a breakneck speed, on the basis of 'high inputs, high consumption and

1. Premier Wen Jiabao's speech at Summer Davos in Tianjin, 27 September 2008.

low output', the external dimension of which was the country's huge dependence on exports.

- The second stage (2005-late 2008) was marked by a fundamental shift in the direction of country's development strategy—from the hitherto followed, 'GDP centric approach' to that aimed at achieving 'balanced development'. Accordingly, boosting domestic demand became a new priority, along with a corresponding change externally providing for reduction of dependence on exports. This shift in basic objectives has been reflected in China's Eleventh Five-Year Plan (2006-2010), formulated in 2005. Also, in the matter of attracting foreign direct investment (FDI) to the country, a significant policy change was noticed in this period; investment emphasis was shifted from 'quantity' to 'quality'.
- The current third stage, which began in November 2008, a period when the impact on China from the global financial crisis became heavy, is notable for two features. Firstly, the authorities are no longer mentioning the need to 'prevent economic overheating and curb inflation', stressed since the beginning of that year. Instead, 'maintaining growth through expanding domestic demand', is now being propagated as the aim. The jettisoning of the concept of 'overheating prevention' and its replacement by that of 'expansion of domestic demand' appears to be significant in the context of changed domestic economic situation as a result of the global financial crisis. The second point appears even more important. Some signs of China's new interest in shaping future international economic arrangements have surfaced in this period, which mark a departure from the past strategy of veteran leader Deng Xiaoping which indicated a low profile for China in global affairs, while developing its economy. Notable in this regard would be the opinions expressed by the People's Bank of China Governor Zhou Xiaochuan (March 2009) on establishing a 'new world reserve currency', to be built on the IMF's Special Drawing Rights (SDRs), as a replacement of the US dollar. Coupled with Premier Wen's expressions of some worry about the safety of Chinese assets in the US and support to diversification of the PRC's reserves, Zhou's

remarks are suggestive of China's growing dissatisfaction of China with the existing US-led world economic order, and Beijing's intentions to play from now on a proactive role in bringing in a 'just and equitable' international order.

Energy Factor

In tracing the link between China's domestic development goals and its external foreign economic relations, the energy factor naturally assumes special significance. In the prevailing situation marked by a big gap between the resources supply and demand at home, a fast developing China would need more and more resources from abroad. Reflecting recognition of this requirement, the PRC's official documents have declared energy security as 'centrepiece' of China's foreign policy.[2] China's resource diplomacy aimed at tapping world energy supply sources, now covers the entire globe—the Middle East, Central Asia, Russia, Africa, Latin America and the Asia-Pacific.

China's resource diplomacy is undoubtedly a crucial component of its external economic relations. For the rest of the world, assessing the significance of prominent trends in that diplomacy has become important in the matter of their addressing the question of how to respond to them. First, Beijing is making it clear that the PRC's future energy policy direction will concentrate on diversifying the supply sources as a response to its perceived vulnerability to excessive dependence in this regard on the politically volatile major energy centres of the Middle East and Africa. The emerging alternative energy sources for China include four areas—Latin America, domestic locations with oil and gas potentials, off-shore zones and land territories nearer home like Russia and Asia-Pacific. China is seeking to help build in Asia-Pacific connectivity through projects such as construction of a canal across the Kra Isthmus in Thailand linking the Indian Ocean to the Pacific coast, the Irrawaddy corridor in Myanmar, connecting it with Yunnan province and Gwadar port in Pakistan to link Xinjiang with the outside world through the Karakoram highway.

Second, there are clearer indications than ever of China's preference for building overland oil and gas pipelines. An important contributing

---

2. Hsiao (2008).

factor is its recognition of the potential security problems in oil transport through distant sea lanes and the inadequacy of its Naval strength to protect such sea lanes. Beijing's plans for developing land pipeline routes (e.g. China's pipelines connecting Kazakhstan, Myanmar and Russia) explain this trend. Reducing dependence on sea borne energy trade, especially through the Malacca Straits, appears to be an important objective. About 80 per cent of China's oil imports pass through piracy-ridden and maritime terrorism-prone straits. Besides, this is a crucial maritime location which the US and its allies are trying to dominate through joint naval exercises, as well as programmes such as the Container Security Initiative (CSI), Proliferation Security Initiative (PSI), and the Regional Maritime Security Initiative (RMSI). China's fears are that such a vital energy supply channel could be cut at times of conflict.[3] President Hu Jintao described this as China's 'Malacca Dilemma'.

A third trend relates to the modification of China's stand towards 'rogue' states like Iran, Sudan and Myanmar since 2006. The three are important energy exporters to China, but of late Beijing is less hesitant than before, to criticise them on issues such as their nuclear programmes, human rights and democratic reforms. Interestingly, the US has been appreciative of such a changed approach on the point of Beijing, especially on the Darfur issue relating to Sudan.[4] This modification appears to be essentially a shift in diplomacy taken in China's national interest,[5] and not a fundamental change in its traditional position of extending economic assistance and arms aid to 'rogue' regimes in return for the latter's energy supplies. In any case, it appears to have come about in response to the felt need to neutralise Western criticisms of China's 'non-interventionist' policy towards such states, ignoring their poor human rights records, which it has followed hitherto.

Fourth, China's traditional mercantilist approach towards procuring energy supplies from abroad is changing. So far China has sought to lock up energy resources around the world, by gaining outright ownership of the production bases located in key countries. The West on the other hand has

3. Xuegang (2008); Zhenjiang and Baoan (2007).

4. China Daily (2007); China Security Journal (2008).

5. Kleine-ahlbrandt and Small (2008).

taken an opposite stand, favouring a liberalised world energy market with competition between nations on a level playing field. Reflecting policy changes, China's expressed preference of the option of outright takeovers is slowly giving way to that of favouring long-term contracts for crude supplies. Evident in this regard is China's desire to avoid any 'zero-sum energy competition' with other powers like the US and Japan.[6]

Fifth, China is making use of the recent fall in oil prices in the global market conquest on the ongoing financial crisis to acquire energy assets abroad with the support of resource-based financing from its other banks. Acquisitions already made in this way included the buying by China National Petroleum Corporation (CNPC) of Canada's Tanganyika Oil venture in Syria and the China Aluminum Corporation's (CHALCO) getting 18 per cent share in the Australian mining company Rio Tinto.[7] This gives rise to a feeling that China is seeking alternative places to park its trade surpluses in order to reduce its over-exposure to the US, indicated by its heavy investment in the US Treasury bonds.

Lastly, there is growing evidence that China is beginning to bring into play the support of the People's Liberation Army Navy (PLAN) to protect the country's maritime interests. In January 2009, for the first time since the founding of the PRC in 1949, three PLA naval vessels took part in a UN sanctioned anti-piracy operation off the Horn of Africa. Also, vessels retired from the Navy are increasingly being pressed by China to patrol disputed South China Sea Islands and the Senkakus claimed by Japan.[8] At policy levels, the PRC's defence documents have noted the need for the armed forces to get involved in ensuring the country's energy security, for e.g., its *Defence White Paper* (2006) referred to the 'ongoing attempts to expand the range of PLA Navy and Air force' and 'mounting security issues relating to energy resources'. The 2008 *Defence White Paper* elaborated these ideas by referring to 'the intensifying struggle for strategic resources'. Also there are increasing official references to the PLA's undertaking of

6. Statement of Mikkal E. Herberg, Research Director, Asian Energy Decurity Programme, before the US-China Economic and Security Review Commission, 14 June 2007.
7. Ford (2009).
8. Storey (2009a and 2009b).

'historic long term missions of a non-war character',[9] for protecting China's territorial and maritime interests through acquiring aircraft carriers, next generation weapons etc.[10]

A word about implications for India arising from China's energy hunt abroad would be appropriate. It is natural for China and India to compete in accessing overseas resources and their targets are almost the same resource-rich regions, particularly their respective neighbourhood, offering advantages in terms of logistics and cost (Iran, Bangladesh and Myanmar for India, and Russia, Central Asia and Myanmar for China). It would be important for New Delhi to watch for the likely commercial and strategic impact of Beijing's resource diplomacy on India and formulate suitable responses. On the whole, Beijing's strategy of mixing its overseas energy search with trade, aid, diplomacy and arms sales has worked very well; this point should not be missed by India, whenever it seeks to tap resource-rich nations. A factor which could compel India to respond strategically relates to indications of China developing military capabilities for use in conflicts over natural resources located in disputed territories in the region and investing in military programmes designed to improve 'extended range projection'.[11] As energy supply requires connectivity, Beijing has also put in place a 'string of pearls' strategy to link China and the oil sources in the Middle East traversing India's neighbourhood. China is also trying to increase its military and economic ties with South American countries and to increase its control in the Indian Ocean, a vital transit route for energy import sources from the Middle East and Africa.

A study of China's position on leading international economic issues and its implications should be the basis of any attempt to come to large conclusions on China's foreign economic policy.

Global Financial Crisis

Foremost is the question of how the PRC views the global financial crisis. In the government's perceptions, China's 'external economic

9. Beijing Review (2009).
10. China Daily (2009).
11. US Department of Defense (2009); Fravel (2007).

environment has become more problematic, and uncertainties have increased significantly'.[12] On the causes behind the financial crisis, Beijing tends to blame the West. Premier Wen Jiabao articulated this thought prior to attending the G20 summit. In his words, the crisis has been due to the 'inappropriate macroeconomic policies of some economies and their unsustainable model of development, characterised by prolonged low savings and high consumption; it fully exposed the deficiencies in the existing international financial system and its governance structure which is required to be tackled through international cooperation'.[13] Wen's critical stand on the West, is also reflected in his demand for the establishment of a new world economic order, opposition to trade protectionism and call on the international community, particularly the developed countries, to assume responsibilities and obligations to minimise the damage caused by the crisis.[14]

Beijing considers that the 'current crisis has had a rather big impact on China's economy and lists the challenges before the country as shrinking external demand, overcapacity in some sectors, difficult business conditions for enterprises, rising unemployment in urban areas, great downward pressure on economic growth and resurgence of trade protectionism'.[15] Confirming such views, the Chinese official statistics reveal that for the first time in five years, China had a single digit growth rate of 9 per cent in 2008 and for the first quarter of 2009, the rate declined further to 6.1 per cent, the lowest in two decades. The World Bank on its part has estimated a 7.2 per cent growth for China in 2009.

The PRC has reacted promptly to the crisis. At policy levels, the Chinese government has started to readjust its macroeconomic strategy, and implement a proactive fiscal policy along with a moderately relaxed monetary policy.[16] Putting the policy into action, it announced a US $586 billion construction-focussed stimulus package in November 2008, aimed at realising the broad objectives of economic restructuring and promoting

12. Premier Wen Jiabao's address at National People's Congress, Beijing, March 2009.
13. Premier Wen Jiaobao's speech at World Economic Forum, Davos, 28 January 2009.
14. Ibid.
15. Second Session of the Eleventh National People's Congress (NPC), 13 March 2009.
16. Premier Wen Jiabao's speech at Boao Forum for Asia (BFA) Annual Conference, April 2009.

growth potentials to spur demand and consumption. The priority areas of the package included low-income housing, rural infrastructure, water and electricity. At the beginning of February 2009, the PRC State Council unveiled plans to strengthen 10 'pillar' industries that have been most affected by the current crisis including the automobile, steel and shipping sectors. These are regarded as particularly significant from the point of view of China's perceived need for external support to such sectors.[17]

Beijing has noted the 'positive' signals emerging from the initial results of the government's initiatives; not to be missed is the point that such signals appears to be stronger in the interior provinces in Central and Western China, as compared with coastal provinces. By March 2009, industrial output picked up to 8 per cent from the 3 per cent level of previous months.

China's Foreign Reserves

The PRC's foreign reserves are now estimated to be around US $1.95 trillion. Its external assets are mostly in US Treasury bonds. As the global financial crisis deepened, concern has been expressed in China, voiced notably by Premier Wen Jiabao,[18] about the safety of Chinese assets in the US. This seems to be based on fears that massive spending spree by the US could undermine the values of Treasury assets to the detriment of China's interests. Washington has promptly tried to dispel such fears. Considering the sensitivity of the subject in the context of the US economic recovery, Secretary of State Hillary Clinton, during her China visit, requested the PRC to continue buying US bonds. President Obama himself gave an assurance that the Chinese assets would be safe in the US.

There is authoritative opinion in China favouring a diversification of the investment of Chinese reserves. At the same time, there seems to be no immediate likelihood of Chinese withdrawal from the US bond market. Beijing's expression of hope that a stable US dollar exchange rate will be maintained appears to confirm this.[19] The situation is however fluid, with

17. Clyde V. Prestowitz, President, Economic Strategy Institute, Testimony before the US-China Economic and Security Review Commission, 24 March, 2009.
18. China Digital Times, 24 June 2009.
19. Wall Street Journal (2009).

China taking precautionary measures e.g. providing for carrying out foreign trade in Asia by its five designated cities (Shanghai, Guangzhou, Shenzhen, Zhuhai and Dongguan) in yuan, instead of the US dollar or any other major world currency. Such steps decoupling China's exports from the US dollar and increasing its influence in emerging markets could be strong indicators of a new stage of the global financial crisis, in which the major countries will use their currencies, economic and political muscle, and implicitly military strengths to carve out a larger share in a new division of the world economy.[20]

Yuan Convertibility

On various occasions, the authorities in China have expressed the government's commitment to make the yuan a fully convertible currency. Some foreign leaders have also visualised the possibility of such a development, e.g. the Russian Finance Minister has said (7 June 2009) that the yuan could become a fully convertible world reserve currency in 10 years. A managed floating exchange rate regime, pegged against a basket of currencies was introduced by China in 2005. There are opinions outside China that Beijing is not rigorous in implementing this regime. Fears are also being expressed that a steady depreciation of the yuan may lead to pressures for depreciation of other Asian currencies, which could destabilise regional financial markets.[21] While the yuan remains non-convertible, the PRC has concluded a number of currency swap agreements (worth about US $95 billion), with major trading partners like South Korea, Argentina and Indonesia, thereby widening the use of the yuan outside China. This could be a significant pointer to China's future policy.

A convertible yuan is certain to impact on the rest of the world. Some experts are of the view that, 'If after a trial period, China makes its currency convertible, the consequence is that importing countries must have reserves of yuan. To get them, Central Banks around the world will have to divest themselves of US assets and Treasury bonds. The Euro has a rather limited role in Asian exchanges. The massive levels reached by the foreign debt of the United States and excessive and unjustified devaluation

20. *Asia News* (website), 1 January 2009.

21. Yiping (2009).

of China's yuan are two high-risk factors for the world economy and stability.'[22] A devaluation of the yuan *vis-à-vis* the US dollar, may have disastrous effect on China's exports. Factories would have to shut down and workers would face lay-offs. This is likely to have serious implications for the legitimacy of the ruling Chinese Communist Party (CCP). Also likely to be affected in that event are foreigners who have invested heavily in China.

China's Role in the WTO

Since China became a member of the WTO in 2001, it has been correct in implementation of WTO commitments in many areas like tariff reduction and elimination of import licences. However, the PRC's laws and practices tend to disregard WTO's principles including the most basic e.g. on 'national treatment' and 'protection of intellectual property rights'. Regarding the Doha round of negotiations, China's stated policy is to 'support efforts to achieve early and balanced results, play a constructive role and deepen the foreign related economic structural reform including through creation of a better environment for foreign businesses in China.'[23] China is however coming under criticism for not engaging hard enough to find a compromise on the Doha round. China needs to deregulate restrictions on foreign financial institutions, and to liberalise its financial market, but the lingering shadow of its planned economy may come in the way of financial sector development.[24]

Foreign Trade

Over the last two years, there has been a falling trend in China's exports and imports. In 2008, the total trade volume reached US $2.56 trillion, a growth of 17.8 per cent year-on-year, but for the first time that foreign growth rate dropped below 20 per cent. In the first five months of 2009, China's exports fell by 21.8 per cent.[25]

---

22. *Asia News* (website), 1 January 2009.
23. Premier Wen Jiabao's speech at Summer Davos in Tianjin, 27 September 2008.
24. Eundak (2007).
25. China's Customs Statistics, May 2009.

China's trade surplus, however, remains substantial. In end of April 2009, it stood at US $75.43 billion, for the sixth straight month. According to the PRC State Council, falling exports are the biggest challenge for the Chinese economy.[26] Many enterprises have already been forced to close down, particularly in the export reliant industrial sector throwing out about 8.7 million people out of jobs.[27] There is also an indication of increasing fear in China of damages to its export industry as a result of intensified protectionism from its major trading partners, a trend increasingly being noticed in China. The issue of protectionism was discussed when US Treasury Secretary Timothy Geithner visited Beijing in the beginning of June 2009.[28]

New policy initiatives being taken by the end of May 2009 to boost exports have included tax-breaks, expanded credit insurance and more accessible financial aid. Short-term export credit insurance to trading companies dealing with high-tech and intensive industries has been notable.

China's announcement of a 'buy Chinese' policy in June 2009 could affect its foreign trade relations, as it stipulated that only Chinese products and services maybe used for government procurement, excepting for certain products which are not available within the country, or could not be bought on reasonable commercial or legal terms.[29]

Foreign Direct Investment (FDI)

The global financial crisis is influencing the flow of FDI into China. In 2008, the FDI into China was US $92.4 billion, a growth of 23.6 per cent compared to the previous year. But the rate of increase is slowing as against the inflow in previous years.[30] China's remedial measures in this regard have included streamlining of procedures for FDI approval, channelling more FDI to China's central and western regions, boosting

---

26. Bloomberg News (2009).
27. People's Daily (2009).
28. *www.chinatrade.com/blog*, dated 24 June 2009.
29. *www.china-briefing.com/news*, dated 17 June 2009.
30. *Xinhuanet* (2009).

investment in high-tech industry and transferring FDI approval rights to government departments at lower levels. A new anti-monopoly law was introduced in August 2008 but it is found by foreign investors as one discouraging them from bidding for local companies. It is alleged by them that the law is a symbol of increased protectionism on the part of China. Other concerns on the part of foreign countries pertain to the exclusion of overseas businessmen, or confinement to a minority participation in the sensitive and strategic sectors of the economy. To improve the FDI climate, there is a pressing need for Beijing to address such concerns.

Also of interest, is the movement towards increasing Chinese investment abroad. Beijing's announcement of the issue of dollar denominated bonds by non-financial firms at home is expected to help China-based companies, particularly those dealing with resources procurement and high technology to invest abroad, making use of such bonds.

Regional Cooperation

China's policy of active engagement in the regional integration process is an integral part of its strategy of 'peaceful development'. The principles laid down by China for regional cooperation comprise 'cooperation in international affairs, strengthening of trade and economic cooperation, firm opposition to trade protectionism, promotion of construction of Free Trade Zones and cooperation in the fields of finance, investment and environmental protection'.[31]

The Asia-Pacific region remains the main theatre of China's regional cooperation. China wants to ease potential tensions and fears among other Asian nations by joining international regimes and following global norms. Beijing's stated vision is to establish 'harmony' in that region; to achieve this, it has proposed a regional cooperation concept featuring 'equality, mutual benefit, openness and practicality' and according 'due role' to ASEAN. In China's view, in parallel to the pursuit of such cooperation, the existing regional and sub-regional cooperation mechanisms needs to be developed further. Seeking to explain its 'harmony' goal above in strategic

31. Premier Wen Jiabao's speech at Boao Forum for Asia (BAF) Annual Conference, April 2009.

terms, the PRC thinks that, 'peace is a product of parity, balance of power and offensive and defensive strengths' and that no action should be taken sacrificing interests of one country while protecting those of other nations. In the security context, it believes that 'missile defence partnerships in some areas would be detrimental to strategic balance, confidence building and regional stability'. China emphasises the 'non-exclusive' nature of regional cooperation, drawing on the development practices of other regions.

In the framework of the vision outlined above, China is working towards finalising bilateral trade deals and free trade agreements (FTAs) with its strategic partners. In 2002, China and the ASEAN signed the framework agreement on comprehensive economic cooperation, providing for establishment of China-ASEAN Free Trade Area (CAFTA) by 2010. Other notable agreements concluded include China-Pakistan agreement on trade in services (February 2009), China-Peru FTA (November 2008), China-Singapore FTA (2008) and China's trade deals with Senegal, Chile and New Zealand (all in 2008). China's free trade negotiations with Australia, India and Gulf Cooperation Council (GCC) are in progress. Also under consideration is a China-Taiwan Economic Cooperation Framework Agreement (ECFA). China has supported the leading role of the ASEAN plus 3 in both the ASEAN regional community building and the East Asia Summit mechanism. To fight the global economic crisis, South Korea, China, Japan and the ASEAN nations agreed in October 2008 to create a US $80 billion fund.

A study by the Asian Development Bank on China's role in regional integration has been cautiously optimistic by observing that the CAFTA is expected to benefit the richer members of ASEAN such as Malaysia and Singapore rather than poorer members like Cambodia. In its view, the PRC and ASEAN are acting in their own respective geopolitical interests through CAFTA.[32] In the case of CAFTA, security ramifications, rather than economic benefits, appear to be the main consideration for China.[33] It is also assessed by some that China lacks confidence in the WTO

32. ADB (2008). *Economics Working Paper Series No.*130.

33. Xiaoyu (2006).

negotiations, and as such, it prefers to engage actively in bilateral, preferential trade agreements.[34]

G2

In January 2009, US experts including former Secretary of State, Henry Kissinger and former National Security Advisor, Zbigniew Brzezinski urged the incoming Obama administration to raise US relations with China to a higher level. Brzezinski, considered close to President Obama, has called for setting up of an informal G2 mechanism between the US and China.[35] Also, the US Secretary of State Hillary Clinton, while visiting Beijing, echoed the same feelings by signalling movement towards an enhanced level of engagement with China, taking the form of a 'strategic and economic dialogue', in place of the 'strategic economic dialogue' pursued by US treasury secretary, Henry Paulson. In the same context, the comments of British Foreign Secretary David Miliband also appear important. He has stated (17 May 2009) that, 'China will be an indispensable world power in 21st century with a decisive say on future global economy and that it will be one of the two world powers that could count along with the US.'

The G2 proposal seems to be based on a fact that China is the largest creditor of the US and the US is China's biggest export destination. The strong interdependence between the two economies therefore provides a foundation for joint action that can shape the global economy. The G2 proposal has however come under criticism of other scholars who feel that it is impractical, as it only represents mismatched interests, values and capabilities between the two. Thus, China's need for resources and markets, clashes with the Western goals of improving human rights and governance in the developing world.[36]

While there has been no official response from China to the G2 proposal, an article, in the State-controlled press,[37] noted the G2 proposal

34. "Bridging Multiple Divides", Paper presented at the annual meeting of the International Studies Association's 49th Annual Convention, USA, March 26, 2008.

35. Brzezinski (2009).

36. Economy and Segal (2009).

37. Pamlin (2009).

with a comment that, 'while most people are looking for a US-China G2, the most important G2 will probably be that of China and India. We should see these two in a relationship that is mutually beneficial'. A subsequent blog in the Chinese official media while referring to G2, pointed to the existence of a pro-US lobby in China, which could welcome the proposal.[38] It is a plausible surmise that China may not be enthusiastic about the G2 proposal due to its geopolitical implications. Beijing may realise that an US-China 'alliance' of this type may cause misgivings among the surrounding Asia Pacific nations and also may not be popular in the Islamic world.

Conclusion

Notwithstanding the indicators identified above of China's new interests in shaping the future international economic system, it is doubtful whether Beijing will be willing to make concrete moves forward in this regard, at least in the short and medium-term. The PRC is still too weak player to influence international economic institutions, which remain US-dominated. Till China can achieve the stated goal of becoming a medium level developed nation (i.e., by 2050), its priority will continue to be domestic development. Confirming this approach, Singapore's Minister Mentor Lee Kwan Yew, expressed this view that Chinese leaders want minimal disruption in the status quo in the world order led by the US, as they need to concentrate on building the country's economic, military and diplomatic strength, and that China is not yet ready to be another world pole.[39] Regarding the world financial system, with US recovery looking distant, it would now be the responsibility of the international community to restore order, the G8 discussions (July 2009) have highlighted this point. China's possible moves to diversify the investment of its reserves and inclination towards finding an alternate world reserve currency will need to be watched closely. Taking the Chinese economy as a whole, the indication is that much would depend on external demand. Beijing has officially

38. Liu (2009).

39. Straits Times, Singapore, 10 April 2009, quoting from Lee Kwan's speech on 9 April 2009.

admitted this against the background of continuing shrinkage in foreign trade and surge in the country's fixed assets investment.[40] The government's stimulus package has no doubt led to some economic recovery, but as officially acknowledged, 'uncertainities still exist in the face of falling export demands and sluggish industrial growth.'[41] Under such circumstances, the expectation that the contribution of China (along with India), both of which has been relatively less affected by the global economic crisis, will be an active factor in world economic recovery, appears to have no firm basis.

40. China's General Customs Administration Bulletin, 12 May 2009, *www.chinaview.cn*, (accessed 14 May 2009).

41. People's Daily online, 27 July 2009.

References

Beijing Review (2009). "Naval Ambitions", 18 May, quoting Admiral Wu Shengli.

Bloomberg News (2009). "China Sees Grim Job Market, Deeper Impact from Global Crisis", 3 June.

Brzezinski, Z. (2009). "A Group of Two that could Change the World", *Financial Times*, 13 January.

China Daily (2007). "US Envoy Defends China's Role in Darfur", 12 April.

———. (2009). "China says Navy Expansion No Threat to Others", quoting PLA Navy Deputy Chief Maj Gen Zhang Deshun, 25 March.

China Security Journal (2008). "Energy Security and UN Diplomacy", 4(3). Summer.

Economy, Elizabeth C. and Adam Segal (2009). "The G2 Mirage: Why the US and China are not Ready to Upgrade Ties", *Foreign Affairs*, May/June.

Eundak, Kwon (2007). "Financial Liberalisation in the PRC: Challenges of Establishing a Market Oriented Financial System", Department of Political Science, SW Minnesota University. Paper presented at annual meeting of the International Studies Association (ISA) 48th Annual Convention, Chicago, USA, February 28.

Ford, Peter (2009). "China Taking Advantage of Global Recession, Goes on a Buying Spree", *Christian Science Monitor*. 21 February.

Fravel, M. Taylor (2007). "China's Search for Military Power", MIT, National Institute of Defence Studies Symposium, Tokyo; (2008). *The Washington Quarterly* 31(3): 125-41. The Center for Strategic and International Studies and MIF.

Hsiao, Russel (2008). "Energy Security: Centerpiece of China's Foreign Policy", Report on Foreign Relations in 2008, *China Brief* 8(16). The Jamestown Foundation. 1 August. Quoting Wen Weipo of Hongkong.

Liu, Henry C.K. (2009). "Brzezinski 's G2 Grand Strategy", *China Daily*, 27 June.

Pamlin, Dennis (2009). "A New G-2 in Asia to Help Steer the Way", *China Daily*, 21 April.

People's Daily (2009). "China Sees Some Recovery in Employment: More Efforts Needed", State Council. 4 June.

Stephanie Kleine-ahlbrandt and Andrew Small (2008). "China's New Dictatorship Diplomacy", *Foreign Affairs* 87(1). Council of Foreign Relations. January/February.

Storey, Ian (2009a). "'Impeccable' Affair and Renewed Rivalry in South China Sea", *China Brief* 9(9), 30 April.

———. (2009b). "Two Chinese Maritime Survey Ships Patrolled Senkakus on 8 December 2008 and March 2009", AFP, 15 March.

US Department of Defense (2009). "The Military Power of the People's Republic of China, 2009", Annual Report to Congress. Office of the Secretary of Defense, US. p.14.

Wall Street Journal (2009). "FOCUS: G8 Unlikely To Examine Dollar's Reserve Status", quoting China's Vice Foreign Minister He Yafei, 8 July.

Xiaoyu, Pu (2006). "China's Adaptation of Foreign Policy towards Asian Regionalism", *International Studies Association (ISA) Paper*. March.

Xinhuanet (2009). "China's FDI up 23.6% in 2008", 15 January.

Xuegang, Zang (2008). "China's Energy Corridors in Southeast Asia", *China Brief* 8(3). 31 January. The Jamestown Foundation.

Yiping, Huang (2009). "China's Exchange Rate Policy Dilemma", *East Asia Forum*. 22 February, *www.eastasiaforum.org*

Zhenjiang, Fan and Ma Baoan (eds.) (2007). *Junshi zhanlue lun*. Beijing: Defence University Publishing House.

7 India-China Economic Relations

Vivek Bharati

India's approach to economic relations with China has seen an evolution over the last two decades. There have been ups and downs, in the sense that beginning with some indifference in the early 1980s, when we did not really take notice what was going on in our neighbourhood, particularly the significance of China's launching its programme of economic reforms, we have, over the years, evolved a better and more mature understanding as well as closer engagement. This actually began with Rajiv Gandhi's visit in the late 1980s. Thereafter we got absorbed in our own reforms and nothing much happened, but subsequently in the late 1990s, we entered an era of surprise, shock and awe at what was going on in China. This was particularly so because of the realisation dawning on us that China was rising rapidly on the economic front. There was even some alarm at this development but subsequently, as we now also began growing at a higher rate over the last 7-8 years that alarm has subsided. There is much more confidence now in our own abilities, but even so, we do retain a schizophrenic approach towards China, in the sense that there is this huge desire, and when I say we, I am including everybody, including the business sector, to exploit the opportunity which this huge, burgeoning economic juggernaut offers to the world and, of course, to us. But at the same time we are extremely wary of its competitive might and the disruptive force in the global economy which it has come to represent. Nonetheless, it is noteworthy that bilateral India-China trade is the fastest growing component in our respective trade baskets. Further, the pace has accelerated in the last 3-4 years and the bilateral trade target of $40 billion set during President Hu's visit three years ago, has been greatly exceeded. Dr. Charan Wadhwa mentioned the figure of US $58 billion dollars; perhaps US $52 billion was the latest figure, and this is nearly 30 per cent more than the target set three years ago.

At the same time, this rapid increase in trade is also becoming a cause for concern. I have just read the recent statement by our Ambassador in Beijing, referring to the huge trade imbalance, (i.e., a deficit of over $10 billion), which is staring us in the face. We have officially expressed our displeasure at this burgeoning trade deficit. The issue is whether this will cause increasing bilateral friction in the years to come, or will this be seen as a game which is of mutual advantage i.e., will it create trust or will it create disruption? This is one issue that I would like to leave on the table. I do think that the trade deficit is likely to continue to rise for the simple reason that this is actually built into the structure of the two economies. When we look at the composition of the two trade baskets, it becomes clear that nearly 60 per cent of our export to China is dominated by primary or very low labour intensive products. Perhaps, the one exception would be value added manufacture, e.g. specialty chemicals. Apart from that, our export basket is primitive, as measured by the stature that we aspire to on the global economic stage. As against this, China's export basket is hugely diversified and reflects its diversified manufacturing base, and comprises both labour and capital intensive items. So, it is not only Chinese toy exports that disturb us, but the fact that it is increasingly high-tech and high value added items are being exported by China. So, it is the entire manufacturing spectrum. So, in a way this really reflects the structure of the two economies. India's manufacturing sector despite a decade and half or two decades of reform, remains inward looking. Whereas China started with this huge export orientation and that is what created their manufacturing base. So, the two strategies have been different and that is what is reflected in the trade basket. The preponderance of trade in China's GDP (i.e. Trade GDP Ratio) is overwhelmingly large than ours. (Three times China has established itself as an aggressive globaliser, and will from all indications continue to be a very dynamic exporter of manufactured products. A point that needs to be stressed here is that when we examine the evolution of the two export baskets of China and India, we find that export structure has not changed much. Indeed, the share of manufactured exports in our overall trade basket has gone down; this is not surprising because petroleum exports have come to dominate the trade basket. This collapsed over the last year, and that is why we are seeing a huge problem in our export turnover. Further, a major item continues to dominate our export basket—i.e., gems and jewellery, which is really a low value added item. The other leading items are textiles and apparel, and increasingly, primary products such as iron-ore and cotton. This makes it clear that we are not a manufacturing exporter. This point needs to be absorbed and accepted, when we talk about trade deficits. On the other hand, China's export mix has been tremendously dynamic. Whereas labour intensive items made up something like two-third of the export basket in 1991-92, today, the share of labour intensive items such as textiles, apparel, and miscellaneous labour intensive products such as luggage has really gone down. China today is the biggest world exporter of high-tech items, bigger than the USA. In fact the US suffers a trade deficit *vis-à-vis* China in high-tech items, as defined by the United States itself. This is something that we need to keep in mind—as well as the indication that China's diversification in this direction is likely to continue. The fact is that while we fumble and are unclear about our goals, China is very clear that they want to be the dominant global economic power in the 21st century. They also want to be the biggest source of innovation in the global economy. Their expenditure on R&D over the last decade and half has really increased phenomenally. Today they are the second biggest R&D spender globally, bigger than Japan and Germany, etc. That is what will continue to propel their manufacturing diversification. Let us be fully aware of the significance of these developments.

At the same time, even while the diversification which I have referred to above will continue, the significant point about China and one which makes it truly different from other rising economic powers, is that they are not going to vacate the labour intensive space. They will not vacate the low value added export space, because their cheap supply of labour will continue to be available for the foreseeable future. So, this is perhaps a unique example of a rising power which will continue to dominate all shades of the economic spectrum so to speak, particularly of manufacturing. Thus, they are not likely to yield much space to India in any sector. For example, I do not see India succeeding in exporting apparel or footwear to China, because China will continue to hold to ground in this labour intensive space, even while they become hugely competitive high-tech exporters. Thus, I do not see ourselves being able to find chinks in the

Chinese armour in the manufacturing area. So, my sense is that the trade deficit that is apparently US $10 billion today will continue its rapid rise.

It is said that China's strength is in manufacturing, whereas India's is in services. When one looks at the structures of the two economies, one notes that manufacturing accounts for 50 per cent of GDP in China, while services make up 50 per cent of GDP in India. This is used as an argument that India will be able to close the GDP and export gap with China. This is a false hope, simply because China's dominance of the export scene is huge, and it is in fact a bigger exporter of services than India. We are 8th or 9th on the list of the 10 leading services exporters, and China is a notch or two above us. It is also significant that China has specialised in services which are, in a way, complimentary to its manufacturing prowess in sectors such as shipping, maritime services. This is the kind of space that they will continue to occupy. They are also making rapid strides in IT and IT related enabled services, i.e., in the very sector where we claim special capabilities. If we look at our export basket in services, it is major sector of specialisation and we are globally competitive. It is also the case that in other services we are unlikely to make much of an impact. So, with China catching up in IT and IT enabled services, one does not see, that on the services side India will be able to generate a surplus which is large enough to enable closing the gap in manufacturing. Therefore the trade gap will continue to widen in favour of China as trade goes up rapidly.

The next question is whether the friction, which could be caused by a widening trade gap, be off-set by any kind of mutual advantage in the bilateral economic relationship? The answer depends on how you look at it, and also depends on what you accept and what you do not. On the one hand, there is a tremendous advantage in importing manufactured products from China which are cheaper than from other sources hence our consumers, our infrastructure and our production system gets the advantage. And the fact of the matter is that as India further lower its trade barriers, as it should over a period of time, and particularly after the commitments made at the enduring Doha Round, where manufacturing tariffs etc., would go down further, the size of China's surplus could potentially get bigger. So, the question is should we get used to this, accept it or strive to fight it out and create friction with China on this issue, on a daily basis? This is one issue that we need to think about. On the other hand, and this is the point Ambassador Ranganathan was making, the larger side has less risk in the relationship and China would continue to be a very different player when we look at the Asian economic architecture. It is reassuring to see the trade statistics that India has made it to top 10 among China's trading partners. The indication is that very soon, we could move up i.e., in next few years to this 8th ranking (leaving Russia and Australia behind). However, beyond that, the pace is going to be very slow. We are not about to break into the league of top seven trading partners who have been with China for a very long period of time. Now, the names of the top seven, indicate who China will give importance to in its bilateral economic relationships. It is clear that decade or decade and half, the region that will remain really hugely important for China would be the European Union (EU). Even if EU growth slows down, or is stagnant, they will remain a very large market. The US will also continue to remain a very large market. Then we have this whole regional specialisation in Asia, where a new architecture, a new division of labour has sprung up, with China as its focal point, and everybody from Japan, South Korea, Taiwan, to Singapore, Malaysia and Thailand, are all getting sucked into this division of labour with China. So, these countries will continue to remain very important players as far as China is concerned. So, I do not see India really acquiring the top mindshare as far as China's bilateral economic relations are concerned.

We need to reflect on this both in terms of India, as well as the role we play in South Asia and the efforts that we are making to break into ASEAN and the regional economic architecture, that we were saying we have to be a part of. Of course that is a hope, but the fact is that the architecture has, in a way, already 'happened', and China is its focal point, whereas we are not there. We have an image of China as one of those trade surplus generating countries with which everybody trades. Actually, China has a huge trade deficit with Japan, Korea, and the entire ASEAN. This is because China has become the hub of their exports to the rest of the world. Components and sub-assemblies produced in the ASEAN region, in Japan, in South Korea are exported to China, where value is added, they are put together and then they are exported globally. Thus, China is providing something which is complimentary, and it is now moving aggressively to cement that architecture by creating free trade areas (FTA). The ASEAN

China FTA will become operational in 2010, and this will put pressure on everybody in this area to set up FTAs. Even the US is under this trend of pressure. When Obama went to Beijing there was much talk about what the US will do about ASEAN. Will they offer a free trade agreement to ASEAN? Simply put, from 2010 onwards, US exports to ASEAN will become nine per cent more expensive compared to Chinese exports to ASEAN, and to all the other countries put together. So, Japan will also be under pressure to have an FTA with ASEAN. India is already moving in that direction, and I am sure that it will come into place in 2016-17 onwards, when most of the tariff cuts will come. One will very soon see a China-South Korea FTA, China has already offered an FTA to Taiwan. So overall in this large region we are seeing China moving aggressively, playing the role of a leader. This is a key proposition: China is playing, the role of a leader, in creating a regional economic architecture, and we are merely following in a rather weak way. We are not aggressive about participating in that regional architecture. China's competitive advantage would, actually increase with the development of this regional economic architecture. The FTAs with ASEAN, and the FTAs with South Korea and Japan would increase the competitive advantage of China. So, whether it is China's bilateral trade with India or its regional trading arrangements, the impact on India would be similar. They would continue to remain competitive, maintain the gap on the manufacturing front without allowing much space to India on the services front.

Actually, this is quite a contrast to India's trading pattern in South Asia where we have a surplus with all our neighbours. We do not offer any economic advantage to any of our neighbours of the kind which China is offering to its East and Southeast Asia neighbours. So, that is one contrast that we need to keep in mind. I think the answer is that we have to get our act together. There are no shortcuts in this game and we have to accelerate our own internal reform, we have to accept that China has competitive advantage and we need to catch up. How do we catch up? For this, we own internal systems, we have to reform our labour laws, and taxation laws and much more. Fortunately, some movement is taking place in taxation laws i.e., we have a new Direct Tax Code (DTC) and a new Goods and Services Tax (GST), which is getting pushed in Parliament and that will really move our competitiveness if it gets implemented within a reasonable time. We also need to sharply reduce our fiscal deficit. It is not adequately realised that this really pushes up costs in the system. I will give you an example: Yesterday I got a call from my bank, telling me that I should take a personal loan of Rs. 4 lakh at 17 per cent. The fact is that I have a fixed deposit in the same bank at 6 per cent. This illustrates the point that the cost of capital has to go down dramatically. China has great advantage in capital cost. Now there are other implications of that for China's financial system, which we do not need to get into right now because it is not the subject of our present study. However, the relevant point is that it bolsters their competitiveness.

We also need to reform our university system urgently. The amount of work China has done on its universities and the linkages it has managed to drive with its R&D machine is amazing. We have to just visit China to see what it is doing. Special zones have been created where there are 100 universities, R&D labs, etc., all integrated, feeding into each other with businesses spread out over a thousand acres with infrastructure that even the United States would be hard put to show. So, we are dealing with a different kind of fish here, and we need to recognise that if we have to catch up, that is the goal, perhaps we may do it in our own way, but we need to beat that system as a country, and frankly we have not even started scratching the surface to do what it will take to reach there.

This brings us to the hard-hearted and sorry conclusion that unless we carry out radical reforms in policy and in our work culture, the hope of India being a meaningful part of the Asian economic architecture cannot be realised. That may be an aspiration but we cannot achieve it unless we have aggressive FTAs with that region and that can only happen when we have the confidence that we are competitive. Today we do not have that confidence, and structurally, our export basket does not demonstrate that confidence—regardless of where we trade, i.e., not just with China or ASEAN, but even with the rest of the world. So, unless we really address that issue in all its complexity, we will not be able to become a part of the regional economic architecture.

So, as we look into the future, we have to face some very basic situations. The trade deficit with China will widen and it will become a formidable issue unless we accept it. There is merit in accepting it taking corrective action at home, because to my mind, India is not a leading priority in China's foreign economic policy. Their interests are focussed on East and Southeast Asia in China's neighbourhood, where it seeks of synergy between security and trade interests. This is a fundamentally important point. There is an Asian production chain, of which China has become the focal point and there is vertical integration of production taking place in that region of which we are not a part; China is moving aggressively to consolidate it. The EU and the US, both of which will continue to be the large markets. China's focus will remain these countries with which it is integrating. They arc the commodity exporters which it cultivates, in a very different manner by giving aid, building infrastructure, buying into assets, etc. China's priority would also be the global financial system and its institutions where China seeks an increasing role. We will of course figure somewhere in this scheme, but though we have a fast growing economy, we have not paid sufficient attention to competitiveness and to the role of trade in furthering the advantage that large economies such as India can develop for itself.

8 India-China: Economic Relations

Rajeev Anantaram

Introduction

India and China have been among the world's fastest growing economies for the past decade. China, which initiated wide-ranging reforms in 1978, 13 years before India, has registered average annual growth rates of GDP in excess of 10 per cent for over two decades. This remarkable performance has been approached only by Japan (between 1956 and 1978) and the East Asian tigers during the 1970s and 1980s. China's emergence is remarkable because it achieved these growth rates through a controlled economy, which was systemically different from the countries of East Asia, which were essentially market economies, *albeit* with extensive state direction.

India, which belatedly introduced economic reforms in 1991, motivated by a balance of payments crisis has experienced rapid rates of growth, though the annual average is lower than that experienced by China and also more sporadic. Growth which took off in the early 1990s immediately following reforms, slowed down after a recession that lasted from the late 1990s to 2002, before reviving again in 2003. India's growth rate between 2003 and 2007 was the world's second highest after China and unprecedented in independent India except for the 1950s wherein India experienced rapid growth, *albeit* on a very low base.

India and China which have different development models are here to stay. While China is already the world's third largest economy (measured at prevailing exchange rates) and the second largest when measured in purchasing power parity (PPP) terms. The corresponding numbers for India are 12th and 4th respectively. If the average economic growth rates of major economies this decade are projected over the next three decades, the two countries would be ranked among the world's three largest economies.

The jury is still out on whether the two countries can sustain such stupendous growth over the next two decades, given the likely emergence of structural obstacles along the way. For China, these include rapid domestic resource depletion, which overseas acquisitions can only partially mitigate, environmental stress, in the form of air and water pollution, depletion of forest cover, growing economic disparity, especially spatially, a financial sector that critics allege is not run on sound economic principles, pervasive influence of the state-owned enterprises, in which 'reform' measures initiated during the early 1990s. China scholars are alarmed about the negative impact of one or more of these factors on future Chinese growth.

India also faces the problems as listed above in substantial measures, though the poor development of human capital is an additional, serious constraint to sustained growth. With regard to human capital, measured in terms of education and health and human services, India's performance leaves a lot to be desired. China is far ahead of India, when judged by almost any indicator, and indeed India's performance in the provision of basic social services compares very unfavourably even by developing country standards. It is particularly important for India to improve the quality of human capital because the growth trajectory that India seeks to follow is knowledge intensive. This has been an enforced choice given India's missed opportunities in the 1960s and 1970s to develop labour intensive mass manufacturing as East Asia and China did with great success in beginning of the late 1960s. Knowledge intensive growth will require a critical mass of highly qualified personnel in certain key areas of research and manufacturing, whose growth would generate positive externalities via spillover effects in the rest of the economy.

Regardless of the constraints to growth discussed above, it is clear that China and India are likely to continue to exhibit economic growth rates well above global averages in the foreseeable future. This growth would in turn be manifested in a growing global footprint, especially in the demand and eventual competition for commodities, where China has currently stolen a march over India. The dynamics between these two emerging countries will be watched with increasing interest given its enormous political and economic implications.

This paper focusses on one aspect of economic relationship—trade between India and China. Even a cursory look at the data suggests that

India is far less important to China as a trading partner than vice-versa, but this asymmetry may be expected to narrow considerably over the next decade. India's trade with China is the fastest growing component of its overall trade and is slated to increase further. The converse is also likely to occur though the actual numbers may be far less spectacular, especially given the sheer volume of China's overall trade.

The paper is organised as follows. Section II compares the comparative structures of the two economies, focussing in particular on the drivers of growth. The underlying economic structure goes a long way in determining not just the volume of trade, but also the competitive advantage that a country possesses. Section III seeks to provide some nuance into the trading patterns of the two countries in the context of their overall trading patterns. Section IV concludes.

The Composition of Aggregate Demand in India and China

Until 1980, both India and China were autarchic and inward looking economies, whose sheer weight in numbers allowed an isolationist economic growth model, though with considerable inherent inefficiencies. China, quickly moved towards a more open economic model of growth, based on a combination of necessity and a need for greater technological engagement with the world to overcome technological obsolescence that bedeviled vast sections of the Chinese economy. China, in the years following 1978, has modeled itself on Japan and East Asia, whose economic recovery and subsequent emergence as members of the OECD was initially driven by a strong degree of export orientation.

China's economic growth is largely driven by public and private investment and exports. Domestic consumption is between 20-25 per cent of GDP and has stubbornly remained at that level despite government efforts to induce consumers to spend more.[1] The fact that domestic

1. It must be remembered that the share of domestic consumption in GDP needs to be benchmarked against the sheer size of the Chinese economy. Thus 25 per cent of a $4 trillion economy is as much as $1 trillion, which in absolute numbers is a staggering amount. Annual average GDP growth in China has been approximately 10 per cent, which makes it difficult for consumption growth rates to keep pace, even with added government incentives.

consumption has not taken off, has been ascribed to a variety of reasons, the foremost being the greater perceived need by Chinese citizens to save more for contingencies, or for retirement, following the collapse of the 'Iron Rice Bowl', a cradle to grave welfare system, where the state took care of all social needs from education to health and also post retirement pensions.

Consumption in urban areas, especially in Beijing and along the eastern seaboard has increased sharply but saturating demand in these regions means that demand has to be generated in other regions as well. Central and Western China have not shared the benefits of the Chinese growth story in the Eastern seaboard, and the Pearl River Delta manufacturing hotspots of Guangdong, resulting in vast economic inter-regional disparity, a concern that has been acknowledged by the Chinese government. The government has tried to stimulate rural income by interventionist policies like abolishing agricultural tax, but it is clear that these regions have a way to go before they can match the more developed regions of China in terms of economic prosperity.

Government investment was the principal driver of aggregate demand in the years immediately following reforms. The spending was mostly in the area of infrastructure development and is chiefly responsible for China's advanced state of infrastructure development, at least in certain select areas. These investments were largely intended to be enabling: they served as a strong magnet for foreign direct investment (FDI), which was at the core of China's manufacturing revolution and also strongly helped in the formation of backward linkages in the economy, especially in areas like steel and cement, of which China is the world's largest producer. There is criticism that the Chinese government may well have overdone public investment, especially since it has led to overcapacity in several sectors, made worse by the fact that demand is not as widespread as the Chinese authorities had hoped. However, public investment has now gathered a life of its own and Government investment still remains very high.

Private investment, not very high in the early days of post reform China has picked up considerably, as Chinese private firms are reinvesting a significant proportion of profits, in capacity augmentation, technology purchases, investment in research and development (R&D) or in outright acquisitions of firms abroad. However, exports have been the standout performer in driving China's growth for close to two decades now.

China's switch to an open economy was driven by a serious balance of payments crisis in the mid-1980s, following the depletion in domestic oil production, which in turn resulted in a substantial loss of export earnings. The switch to export oriented mass manufacturing was driven not so much by a need to transform the composition of the domestic economy, but by a more immediate need to generate hard currency. FDI which largely migrated to the Eastern seaboard, for a combination of economic and cultural reasons,[2] helped in the setting up of a vibrant manufacturing sector focussed on the production of low-technology, labour intensive mass manufacturing goods. Within a decade, China was firmly embedded in the world's supply chains and its emergence as the world's factory was a consequence of these developments.

China is currently the world's largest exporter, having overtaken Germany which topped the table for goods and services' exports in 2008. China's exports in 2009 were $1.2 trillion, down 15.8 per cent compared to 2008.[3] Imports were $1 trillion during the same period resulting in a trade surplus of $200 billion, which exceeds the total trade of most countries. The profile of export growth is also interesting. Foreign funded enterprises (FFEs) are major contributor to exports, especially high technology goods accounting for 59 per cent and 85 per cent of the exports respectively. China's global linkages, which translate into a high volume of manufacturing exports, are undoubtedly positive factors, but an artificially undervalued renminbi and government export subsidies, which allow producers to sell at below marginal cost, are other reasons that have also contributed to the export boom. Indian manufacturers have often complained that the price of Chinese manufacturing products is often less than their cost of globally sourced raw material alone! It is not clear what the eventual cost on the Chinese economy of these subsidies will be, but it is self-evident that the cost will have to be borne by someone, most likely by China!

---

2. Most FDI into China in the early days of opening up (post 1980) was by overseas Chinese from Hong Kong and Taiwan. Investments from Hong Kong went to Guangdong province, while Taiwanese investments went to Fujian province. Foreign manufacturing operations were housed in special economic zones (SEZs) mostly on the eastern seaboard and until 1992 all goods manufactured within were exported. Foreign firms were allowed to sell products in the domestic market only after 1992.
3. *Economic & Commercial Report (2009)*, Embassy of India in Beijing.

It is clear that India does not enjoy anything close to the economic leverage that China does, particularly in terms of global penetration of export markets. Aggregate demand in India is driven mainly by domestic consumption, which accounts for about 60 per cent of GDP. Domestic savings have arisen from an annual average of 22 per cent of GDP during the 1990s to 37 per cent of GDP during the boom years of 2004-2007. Investment rates have similarly made a transition from 20-25 per cent of GDP to around 35-37 per cent. The most noteworthy fact is that overall savings and investment rates did not drop below 32 per cent of GDP even during the low point of the recent global turndown, and there are signs that savings and investment are again rising to the levels reached during the boom years. Private investment had dipped during the global slowdown as firms were holding on to the cash they had, and were adopting a wait and watch attitude, but recent reports indicate that private investment is gradually picking up.[4] Public investment, largely in the form of capacity development in sectors such as infrastructure compensated for some of the decline in public investment, but economic recovery in the foreseeable future is likely to see a revival of both public and private expenditure, which could push the total investment rate close to 40 per cent of GDP.

Government spending in India is a larger concern than in China, with the government taking on a high level of debt. The private sector in India has relied on retained earnings to fund investment (between 2004 and 2008). Therefore, government borrowings did not lead to any significant 'crowding out', at least for large firms, though small and medium enterprises did struggle for access to capital. Recent legislation mandating greater financial responsibility does not seem to have had the desired impact as the government is under pressure from diverse interest groups, but high levels of fiscal deficit could act as a drag on the economy, for reasons discussed above.

India's exports have risen sharply since the reforms were enacted, but a long tradition of focussing on a huge domestic market has induced a strategic inertia. The reasons for India's inability to penetrate export markets are numerous, ranging from the lack of competitive advantage from low productivity, widespread technological obsolescence in areas such

4. See Monthly Review of the Indian Economy (CMIE) and Reserve Bank of India annual reports for details.

as textiles and leather, where India's advantages of low-cost labour could have been exploited, an inability to scale up and ascend the value added chain in information technology and manufacturing, lack of a coherent focussed trade policy, among others. As seen in Section III below, India's trade (imports and exports) in absolute numbers is not just embarrassingly low compared to China, but low also relative to other countries in East and Southeast Asia. India's new export policy calls for substantially increasing its global export share, but coordinated policy actions that will combine general and sector specific policies will be needed if India's exports need to be stepped up from the projected $200 billion in 2009, to a figure closer to that of China.

Trade between India and China

As discussed above, China is a far more important player than India in global trade, and is far more important as a trading partner to India than conversely.

Table 8.1

Bilateral Trade Figures: India & China

(US $ billion)

	2004	*2005*	*2006*	*2007*	*2008*	*2009*
India Exports to China	7.67	9.78	10.46	14.65	20.34	13.7
Growth %	80	28	7	40	39	-32.6
China Exports to India	5.92	8.93	14.58	24.03	31.51	29.57
Growth %	77	51	63	65	31	-6.17
Total India-China Trade	13.59	18.71	25.04	38.68	51.85	43.27
Growth %	79	38	34	54	34	-17
Trade Balance for India	1.75	0.85	-4.12	-9.38	-11.17	-15.87

Source: *Economic and Commercial Report for 2009*, Embassy of India, Beijing.

As seen in Table 8.1, above, total trade between India and China has steadily increased from $13.6 billion in 2004 to $43.27 billion in 2009. The peak figure for bilateral trade between the countries was in 2008 when two-way trade between the countries registered its highest figure of $52 billion. The absolute volume of trade has been steadily increasing, though the growth rate has been steady except for the year 2004, when the sharp increase in trade reflected a low volume of bilateral trade in the previous year.

The fall in trade between 2008 and 2009 has been caused more by a decrease in India's exports to China than vice-versa. While India's exports to China dropped by almost a third, China's exports to India have shrunk only by 6 per cent. However, in terms of trade balance, the pattern for India-China showed a different pattern. China's overall (global) trade surplus at $200 billion was 33 per cent lower than in 2008. At the same time, China's trade surplus with India increased from $11 billion in 2008 to $16 billion in 2009 (an increase of 45 per cent).

The fall in India's exports to China could to some extent be explained by the fact that the Chinese economy while growing rapidly, was doing so at a relatively slower pace. Excess capacity in several commodities like cement and steel led to rationalisation measures, especially because domestic demand for these products had slowed down. As seen in Table 8.2, few products in India's export basket to China are high value added. Besides, a wide supplier base for these commodities implies that India's bargaining power is rather limited.

Table 8.2

India's Exports to China by Commodities

HS	*Description*	*Value in US $ Million*		*% Share*		*% Change*
		2008	*2009*	*2008*	*2009*	*2009/2008*
	India	20341.14	13704.07	1.8	1.37	-32.63
26	Ores, slag, ash	14378.25	7968	70.69	58.1	-44.58
52	Cotton yarn, fabric	1131.34	642.19	5.56	4.69	-43.24
29	Organic chemicals	624.94	573.14	3.07	4.18	-8.29
71	Precious stones, metals	417.43	485.3	2.05	3.54	16.26
72	Iron and steel	239.91	441.73	1.18	3.22	84.12
84	Machinery	256.67	413.27	1.26	3.02	61.01
74	Copper+ articles thereof	281.08	408.85	1.38	2.98	45.46
25	Salt, sulfur; earth, stone	363.27	302.83	1.79	2.21	-16.64
39	Plastic	278.52	284.5	1.37	2.08	2.15
76	Aluminium	12.86	257.42	0.06	1.88	1901.64
85	Electrical machinery	216.96	240.68	1.07	1.76	10.93
41	Hides and skins	206.1	166.07	1.01	1.21	-19.42
15	Fats and oils	130	146.68	0.64	1.07	12.83
03	Fish and seafood	93.99	123.55	0.46	0.9	31.45
23	Food waste; animal feed	209.44	109.79	1.03	0.8	-47.58

Source: *Economic and Commercial Report for 2009*, Embassy of India, Beijing.

The top five Indian exports to China during 2009, in order were ores, slag and ash, cotton yarn, organic chemicals, precious stones and metals and iron and steel. These five categories accounted for about 83 per cent of all exports in 2008 and 74 per cent in 2009. While the 'organic chemicals' category includes antibiotics, and thus provides for some value addition, all other products are either commodities or low value added products, in which the labour intensive value addition had already taken place in India. The import of steel was intended to feed the infrastructure boom in China and thus was not specialised steel. For India to penetrate the intensely competitive Chinese market, change its export profile and tap into opportunities that China offers, it would have to produce more value added products, introduce quality control to upgrade product quality and switch to innovation based high-tech products. This would call for a radical and fundamental change of mindset at the level of private sector firms and government.[5]

As shown in Table 8.3, the top five Indian imports from China include, electrical machinery, general machinery, organic chemicals, iron and steel products and iron and steel. These five products cumulatively constituted 68 per cent of Chinese exports to India in 2008 and 71 per cent in 2009. The share of machinery imports into India from China (both electrical and general) increased from 48.7 per cent in 2008 to 55.3 per cent in 2009. The other products included a fairly high share of value addition. Even the category 'iron and steel' consisted more of steel than iron. Indeed, steel imports into India from China included a large component of specialised steel products, though there were also allegations that China was 'dumping' some excess production into India.

The 'electrical machinery' exported by China to India consists largely of capital equipment for the many power projects being undertaken in India. Chinese and Korean electrical equipment manufacturers have obtained several orders to provide equipment, especially for the several

5. These trade statistics do not account for Indian firms that have set up manufacturing operations in China, either through greenfield plants or through acquisitions. The motivation for many Indian firms was to leverage China's vastly superior physical infrastructure, manufacturing environment and be close to potentially the largest market globally. There is no evidence that 'tariff hopping' had much to do with this decision.

Table 8.3

India's Imports from China

HS	Description	Value in US $ Million		% Share		% Change
		2008	2009	2008	2009	2009/2008
	India	31516.47	29570.44	2.21	2.46	-6.17
85	Electrical machinery	8385.33	8775.08	26.61	29.7	4.65
84	Machinery	6963.33	7568.13	22.09	25.6	8.69
29	Organic chemicals	3045.72	2968.8	9.66	10	-2.53
73	Iron/steel products	1200.7	1159.11	3.81	3.92	-3.46
72	Iron and steel	1732.28	593.86	5.5	2.01	-65.72
59	Impregnated text fabrics	568.08	571.69	1.8	1.93	0.64
90	Optics, med. instruments	402.81	547.06	1.28	1.85	35.81
31	Fertilisers	1031.39	519.6	3.27	1.76	-49.62
39	Plastic	597.73	513.42	1.9	1.74	-14.11
87	Vehicles, not railway	563.09	447.05	1.79	1.51	-20.61
50	Silk; silk yarn, fabric	371.9	411.82	1.18	1.39	10.73
28	Inorganic chemicals; rare earth Mt	510.14	392.18	1.62	1.33	-23.12
54	Manmade filaments, fabric	353.65	285.87	1.12	0.97	-19.17
94	Furniture and bedding	260.79	264.3	0.83	0.89	1.35
27	Mineral fuel, oil etc.	832.34	253.06	2.64	0.86	-69.6

Source: *Economic and Commercial Report for 2009*, Embassy of India, Beijing.

private ultra-mega power projects (capacity over 4,000 MW) that are being set up in India. This is a recent development that took place mainly after the electricity sector in India was liberalised through the landmark Electricity Act (2003). Opinions vary on the quality of Chinese electrical equipment, with many Indian producers opting for the more expensive, but also more reliable equipment from western manufacturers, such as Siemens, Alstom, General Electric Corporation etc. However, Chinese equipment is of comparable quality to the one produced by India's largest domestic manufacturer, Bharat Heavy Electricals Limited (BHEL) and considerably cheaper because of the economies of scales Chinese manufacturers have managed to generate.

The Indian government's recent decision to exclude manufacturers who did not have a manufacturing presence in India from bidding in government contracts for equipment has had several foreign manufacturers' expedite plans to set up manufacturing units in India, either as joint ventures with Indian firms or as wholly owned firms. Chinese firms are also part of this process. The implication for trade is that, Chinese exports to India could reduce, since the equipment will now be sourced from domestic production by Chinese firms in India, should they be awarded the contract. Thus, *ceteris paribus*, a decrease in trade could see a corresponding rise in investment.

Concluding Remarks

Despite a greater openness and comfort level between the two countries in recent years, trade and investment between the two countries fall far short of the potential. As discussed, trade between the two countries has grown much faster than investment by each country in the other, with the balance of trade shifting from a slight Indian trade surplus in 2005 to a deficit in 2009. The political leadership in both countries have agreed that the bilateral trade turnover needs to be substantially higher.

However, it is more likely that we could see a trade-investment relationship emerge between the two countries, as opposed to a 'trading only' relationship. Thus, investment could to some extent displace some trade, as seen with the electrical machinery exports of China. India would be a latecomer to the investment scenario in China, given its low current levels of FDI in that country. The situation could change very rapidly, with Indian FDI in China being both 'vertical' and 'horizontal', whereas Chinese FDI in India would be largely horizontal, directed at the domestic market.

Sporadic political tensions between the two countries have not derailed the emerging economic relationship. However, increasing conflict for economic space and resources could unleash a fierce competition, which could potentially result in confrontation. On a positive note, it is also possible that the two countries may simply agree to leverage the economic infrastructure in each other's countries, and in the process develop synergies that both countries could use to their advantage. That would clearly be a gain for both countries.

It is unlikely that the pattern of growth in both countries will change significantly. China will continue to be more outward oriented than India, though it is likely that its citizens may respond more positively to incentives for consumption provided due to greater social security, something which the Chinese government is actively working on. Similarly, India's shift to a more export driven economy will be constrained by structural deficiencies in India's economy and the need to position itself in global markets in line with its own national competencies. However, it is clear that in coming years, both countries will have to incorporate in their global outlook, each other's thinking and requirements.

9 China and the Global Economic Crisis

C.V. Ranganathan

For one who has been a student of developments in China for nearly 50 years, the America-originated global economic crisis presents so many ironies. Right through the 1960s and extending to the 1970s, the US and China were locked in bitter hostility, an American economic embargo was in place and official and non-official relations between USA and China were at a minimum. There was also the political and strategic situation surrounding the American engagement in Vietnam. No China-watcher then would have predicted that by the early years of this century, China would emerge as one of the largest creditors of the USA. Niall Ferguson, the well known Princeton historian remarked after the onset of the global financial crisis, 'usually it is the rich country lending to the poor. This time it is the poor country lending to the rich.' China by 2008 had become the largest buyer of US treasury bonds worth a trillion dollars. In her first overseas tour after she became US Secretary of State, Hillary Clinton was reported to have requested the Chinese during her China visit to continue the purchase of such bonds to help the US recovery plan. Chinese Premier Wen Jiabao delivering the traditional end of session address at the National People's Congress (Parliament) expressed his worry over the risks involved in the huge Chinese investments in USA. President Obama took this up to reassure the Chinese in a Press conference that their investments were safe.

From the mid-1990s China had arguably made possible an American boom. Low cost Chinese goods helped keep a lid on inflation, while the flood of Chinese investments helped the US government finance mortgages and a public debt of close to several trillions of dollars. Then, that government engaged in a costly war in Iraq and Afghanistan, American consumers were encouraged by loose credit to spend on homes and luxury goods and in an easy-money environment, banks created risky new securities, leading to the financial meltdown in late 2008, with its global impact. The huge trade gaps in favour of China, as well as China recycling its trade profits into the USA economy resulted in the closest interdependence between China and the USA, which neither may have wished for. The supreme irony is that when capitalist economies decline, so do their political and economic rivals—China and Russia. The question may well be asked: is it because they are parasitic models of the declining capitalist economy?

If there is a saving grace in the economic crisis currently battering the USA, which also affects China and its past exports dependence on the USA and its vast holdings of US public debt, it would have to come from the same economic interdependence that worries Premier Jiabao. Having for too long lived beyond their means, Americans have become heavily dependent on China to finance the US national debt. China's holds close to US $2 trillion. As China seeks to stimulate its own economy, it will inevitably need to spend more at home and save less, but it would be hurting itself financially if it deviated itself too fast from US holdings. The value of its remaining dollars would plunge, and so would demand for Chinese products in USA. So the need for cooperation is mutual. The two powers will continue to have differences. But they depend so much on each other that they have little choice but to forge commonly acceptable positions to themselves and to the world at large. This was the effort at the G20 meeting of heads of states and governments held in London in 2009.

Going by recent precedents of very major international political and economic developments which took place since the initiation of China's economic reforms in the early 1980s, China has invariably benefited from these developments. A few examples would suffice. The introduction of special economic zones (SEZs) in the southern province of Guangdong, adjoining Hong Kong and Macau was timely as these two capital and technology rich foreign enclaves took advantage of the land, cheap labour and infrastructure facilities offered from across their borders to move their traditional exports oriented industries to China. This marked the beginning of China's export growth after decades of autarchy which isolated China economically from the world. Then came the fall of the erstwhile Soviet Union and Communist regimes in Eastern Europe.

China's answer was to give a further push to reforms, stave off Leftist pleas within the Chinese Communist Party (CCP) for caution and a reversion to orthodox socialist dogmas. Deng Xiaoping argued that the *raison d'etre* of Communist rule was to better the living standards of the population, even if this meant rising inequalities within China. The way to achieve this was to follow what were seen as successful models in East Asia of exports oriented growth. The disintegration of the Soviet hold over its former Central Asian states gave China an opportunity to develop political and economic relations with these resource-rich states. Between 1997-1999 came the Asian financial crisis. China, because of its rather primitive banking structure then and relative limited exposure abroad came out of the crisis unscathed by and large. Its willingness to desist from devaluing its currency *vis-à-vis* the dollar was seen as a responsible step by the international community. China was also quick to come to the aid of countries such as Thailand with impressive loans to tide over its crisis. The question which we must ask is: what is the balance that China will now strike in the face of the present global crisis?

The global financial and economic crisis has had serious consequences for China. Just to mention a few: China's year-on-year growth of foreign trade in 2008-09, dropped by approximately 20 per cent, although its trade surplus still stood at 295 billion dollars. As export markets declined, the manufacturing sector which accounts for 43 per cent of its economy contracted. This in turn worsened an already difficult employment situation. The number of migrant workers from rural areas who have lost their jobs and gone back to their homes which was earlier estimated at 10 million, has doubled since January 2009. One million graduates from universities and institutes of higher learning in 2008 are without jobs and they are expected to be joined by another 6 million by the middle of 2009. The combination of slower exports growth, shrinking imports, rising unemployment, contraction of the manufacturing sector, and rising bankruptcies have cumulatively affected forecasts of China's annual GDP growth. The most optimistic forecast as of present hovers between 5.5 to 6.5 per cent, a significant fall from the double digit GDP growth figures which China has enjoyed for a decade and a half.

To the concerns above in the urban sector, the year 2009 is seen by Chinese economists as the worst year, since 2009 began, for the countryside. For all its past growth centred in the urban areas, agricultural productivity, job training and facilitating the farmer's employment in new public sector infrastructure and other construction projects, in short, improving the livelihood of the majority of the population which lives in the countryside, are the significant problems faced by China now that the earlier paradigms of development have outlived their utility.

Ensuring continuous growth and rising living standards in a socially stable environment has been the *raison d'etre* of the continued existence of the rule by the Communist Party of China. In the context of domestic upheaval in China over the last four decades, the Party has emphasised stability above all other prerequisites for its dominance. Faced with the impact of the externally induced global crisis and international recession, the Chinese government came out with its stimulus package of US $586 billion in November 2008. How this much needed market signal that government is committed to growth will affect the balance between economic growth and social harmony now remains to be seen.

The broad objcctivc of the above package is to facilitate much needed economic restructuring, to make proper use of the growth potential, where it is most needed, such as in rural areas and to spur demand and consumption. In the past, fixed investments and exports gently dwarfed domestic consumption. In what appears to be a linked factor, related to this objective, the stimulus package concentrates on some priority areas: low income housing, rural infrastructure, water, electricity, transportation, the environment, technological innovation, and reconstruction in disaster-hit areas. Encouraging demand in the countryside by various subsidies on consumer durables, enhancing self-employment possibilities through flexible lending policies are corollaries, growing out of these objectives. The instruments through which this basic goal is to be attained, are reforms in value added taxes, abolition of credit ceilings on banks so as to facilitate lending to priority projects, and to small enterprises in rural and urban areas, rationalisation of the industrial set up through restructuring 10 'pillar' industries, mergers and acquisitions, expansion of consumer credit etc. In brief, this involves the adoption of active fiscal, monetary and other policies.

By April 2009, some five months after the announcement of the above package, Premier Wen Jiabao claimed that the government's efforts were bearing fruit e.g., bank lending had risen by record levels, industrial output had picked up to 8 per cent from 3 per cent in the first months of the year, and that urban fixed investment grew during these months supported by a surge in government spending. Wen also cautioned that while initial results from the stimulus plan were encouraging, enormous challenges lay ahead, considering the fact that the collapse of demand for Chinese exports posed a major difficulty.

The onset of the global financial crisis, while highlighting the decline of American economic power and the reliance on China, has also marked a new phase in its global political and economic role. Although such a role was implicit in the immediate past during China's growth phase, the difference now is that the developed countries and China's neighbours in the vast Asian Continent expect China to play a responsible lead role in stabilising the international economic and financial situation. Chinese leaders and high level spokesmen on their part have roundly criticised reckless Western policies for the crisis and have voiced the long held demand of the developing countries for a greater say in the management of international financial institutions. This could signal that China is prepared to take an active and interventionist role in financial affairs, and on issues which affect the world. A bold proposal floated by the Governor of the Chinese central bank is the suggestion for a new global currency to replace the dollar as the reserve currency.

While this proposal may not be taken up seriously for the time being, it is worth noting. This is relevant for growing role of China's currency, the yuan. It remains non-convertible, but China has concluded a number of currency swap agreements, reportedly amounting to US $95 billion with some major trading partners such as South Korea, Argentina and Indonesia thereby widening the use of the renminbi outside China. China is also taking steps to increase the role of the yuan in Hong Kong, and is permitting companies in Southern China to settle contracts with its southern neighbours in yuans rather than in dollars and euros. It has also announced its intention to make Shanghai a global financial centre by 2020, in their meeting preceding the ASEAN Summit of March 2009, (which was aborted on account of the civil disturbances in Thailand), the

ASEAN Finance Ministers agreed to extend the scope of arrangements designed to protect domestic currencies from destabilising swings which could follow the financial crisis in USA. Now the members of ASEAN will have US $120 billion available, on a multilateral rather than on a bilateral basis for the purpose of stabilisation. This was achieved because of the willingness of China, Japan and the Republic of Korea to provide the financial muscle to help their weaker Southeast Asian neighbours. The creation of this regional fund is an expression of discontent with the Asian Development Bank (ADB).

The Chinese have also been quick to turn the international financial crisis into opportunities to acquire holdings of strategically important natural resources such as iron-ore, copper, oil and gas, as well as to build political and economic influence in neighbouring and distant countries. Chinese state-owned corporations which are cash-rich have bought into assets and equities at a remarkable pace in recent months. CHINALCO, the Aluminium Corporation of China, has made an offer to invest US $19.5 billion in Rio Tinto, the major Australian mineral producer. Other Chinese companies have either bought or are proposing to invest in Australian zinc and iron-ore producing companies there. Major deals in the oil and gas sectors have been tied up in Brazil, Venezuela and in Russia. The Brazilian venture would provide China with 100,000 to 160,000 barrels of oil a day, once the Brazilian partner, Petrobras begins exploitation of new and promising off-shore fields. Beijing has also agreed to lend US $15 billion to Rosneft, the Russian oil major, and another US $10 billion to Transneft, a leading Russian pipeline company. These loans would be returned in kind through the export of 3,00,000 barrels a day from the huge Siberian oil fields—over the 20-year life of the deal. China has taken advantage of the fact that now there is a buyers' market for raw materials, and resource companies are struggling to find financiers following the Western banking crisis. China has stepped in vigorously in Latin America, offering countries in the region large amounts of money while they struggle with slowing economies, fall in commodity prices and restricted access to credit. It has offered Venezuela, US $12 billion as part of a development fund, Ecuador, US $1 billion for a hydro power station, and Argentina US $10 billion to enable access to Chinese currency to help pay for imports from China. This arrangement is somewhat similar to those reached with

South Korea, Indonesia and Belarus. China has also become a member of the Inter-American Development Bank (IDB) and will thus now have a role in talks led by the USA to replenish its funds.

American and Japanese automotive manufacturers whose markets at home have collapsed are increasingly looking at China for business opportunities, even as the domestic manufacturing and ancillary sectors are growing; hybrid car production in China is increasing, although costs are high (in an effort to save on fossil fuels). New agreements between the Beijing and Taipei authorities to open up trade, communications, tourism and mutual investments would give a new impetus to trans-Straits relations between Chinese on both sides, cushioning to some extent the global downturn.

Initial reports as of the end of April 2009, seem to indicate some welcome news for the leadership of China. Government figures suggest that overall economic performance may continue to improve during the rest of the year. If true, China may be able to improve living standards and keep down unemployment, which causes social unrest. Economic growth in the first quarter of 2008 was reportedly 6.1 per cent. This is less than the 6.8 per cent recorded for the same quarter last year, but better than what was feared. Industrial output has increased over the same period and, the rate of decline of exports is slower than earlier in the year. However it is the phenomenon of unemployment, and lack of adequate social and health welfare measures, specially in the countryside which is likely to preoccupy the leadership for sometime to come, as this phenomenon affects stability and poses challenges to their credibility.

Eric Hobsbawm, the well known European intellectual, writing recently in '*The Guardian*', the British daily, under the title, 'Socialism has failed. Now capitalism is bankrupt. So what comes next' has this to say: 'A progressive policy needs more than just a bigger break with the economic and moral assumptions of the past thirty years. It needs a return to the conviction that economic growth and the affluence it brings is a means and not the end. The end is what it does to the lives and hopes of peoples... The test of a progressive policy is not private but public, not just rising income and consumption for individuals, but widening their opportunities.' The model of export-led growth for China served it well as long as it could rely on foreign markets, especially those of the developed countries. It led on the one hand to tens of millions being lifted out of poverty, and moving towards becoming consumers of industrial goods. On the other hand, such a model resulted in wide disparities, cut-backs from socialist job and health security, and a rise in corruption, falling moral standards, degraded environment, all in the pursuit of the goal of getting rich quick. Both India and China which are seen as the two large Asian countries capable of surviving (the global economic downturn) with relatively less discomfort need to ponder the lessons inflicted on the developed world and fashion their own solutions to future sustainable growth. These solutions would still involve favouring state over market, especially in the financial sector. This is the case with both India and China, where the development challenge is not the state-market boundary but the far more difficult question: How do you improve the state's own capacity to deliver law and order, security as well as other essential services such as health, water, sanitation and education? This question was relevant before the financial crisis and will remain so in its aftermath.